COME ON CYMRU!
Football in Wales

Keith Haynes

Published by Sigma Leisure – an imprint of
Sigma Press, 1 South Oak Lane, Wilmslow, Cheshire SK9 6AR, England.

British Library Cataloguing in Publication Data
A CIP record for this book is available from the British Library.

ISBN: 1-85058-689-6

Typesetting and Design by: Sigma Press, Wilmslow, Cheshire.

Cover Design: MFP Design & Print

Cover photographs: South Wales Evening Post & Angela Haynes

Photographs: by kind permission of the South Wales Evening Post, except where noted.

Printed by: MFP Design & Print

Preface

This is the first book to be written by fans of Welsh football for football fans everywhere. It offers a brief insight into the Welsh game as it stands today, the rivalries and the statistics, the clubs and the history. Many supporters were given the opportunity to put their club's nostalgia on paper, especially the League of Wales clubs. Some failed to respond or submit their story, and that is their prerogative. Those that have submitted their story now have it in print, something to be proud, of something to show the grandchildren. This book covers the fate of Welsh clubs in Europe, the national side, the demise of Welsh football since the sixties and the hope that it will once again rise from the ashes of its own making. In places it tells a tale, in others it raises a smile.

It also covers one aspect of football that some of us have failed to understand since we first fell in love with the game – the mentality that leads to violence. During my research, I felt this had no place in any football book – I found that there is adequate documentation of this part of our game. I also know, sadly, that it is a part of our game that has failed to go away. So despite my reluctance, it is included, briefly. I was amazed that there are now doctors who have studied football violence and have letters after their name because of it. They have tried to explain the reasons for football violence, but I, like many, will never understand why.

The banter we have all experienced and the happy moments we have all been a part of are included, as well as the tearful times – of which there have been many. Imagine what it is like to find your club relegated to the Vauxhall Conference, to see your team beaten at home by your hated rivals or to recall the very first experiences of football as a young supporter. And many of us were young, impressionable and easily led, when a relative took us to a match for the first time, and unwittingly changed our lives forever – just for the lure of ninety minutes of football! It's all here, and it's all here for the first time. Welsh football as it should be written.

Keith Haynes

Acknowledgements

Thanks to all of the contributors – without them this book would not have been possible. The staff and players of the following clubs have also given invaluable assistance: Swansea City AFC, Cardiff City AFC, Wrexham AFC, Chester City AFC and Hereford United AFC. Thanks also to John Burgum and Jon Wilshire of *The South Wales Evening Post,* and Tony Jenkins of Diff'rent Records. I am grateful to all of the websites that have assisted with publicity, and am particularly indebted to Mouthful of Lead, Gary Martin's unofficial Swansea City pages, Anthil's new Jacksite, Eric the Red's Welsh pages and the Cardiff City, Wrexham, Chester City and Hereford United websites. Finally, my thanks to Graham and the staff at Sigma Press – and, of course, to Brian Stedman for dreaming up the brilliant title!

Tales to tell?

If you have a tale worth telling for future books, send your contributions to:

Ranto Yanto
PO Box 19
Gloucester
GL3 4YA

Contents

Chapter 1

Welsh Football: a country fit for heroes

Keith Haynes

"It's been so, so long. In fact, not in my lifetime."
Ryan Giggs, 1998

Nor in mine, Ryan. In fact, it was five years before I was even deemed a good idea that Wales can claim to have had a team to be really proud of. The Welsh international squad of 1958 battled its way to the World Cup quarter-finals in Sweden, only to go out 1-0 to the eventual winners, Brazil. Since then we have endured failure after failure, near miss after near miss. Oh, how I crave for the failure that Scotland have had in recent World Cups, just for the ninety minutes of hope that we all dream of for our country's 'best' players. You can talk about Rumania at the Arms Park or the dodgy ref at Ninean in 1976. It matters not where we play or who plays for us, we always drop the flowers and end up groping around amongst the feet and stilettos in cold, wet puddles. And what do we get? Bloody trodden on, in fact. The Welsh football supporter has, it seems, almost given up on the national team and concentrated his efforts on either his local side or Manchester United. The latter being the reason why the Welsh game currently lacks support and finds itself in such a mess. Manchester United don't pay the wages at Swansea City or Wrexham, they have lined their pockets well from the trendy punters of today who claim to be football fans. You won't hear Zoë Ball talking about the Cardiff City squad for the 1998-99 football season because she couldn't name you one player in the squad. All she can tell you about Cardiff is it has nice shops and they play rugby . . . don't they?

Football today is no different from what it was twenty years ago. We still play with the same number of players and, near as damn it, to the same set of rules. Refs have changed their garb but then, so have the clubs. The grounds have changed, and rightly so in most respects, but the real fact remains that we still go to watch twenty-two players kick a football around for ninety minutes on a Saturday afternoon because we want to. We go because we care about our clubs. We stand shoulder to shoulder with strangers in all weathers, in the vague hope that City will beat Darlington or Wrexham will beat Preston. Visit these grounds and you will see very little change from twenty years ago. At Ninean the Bob bank survives. A fierce, partisan support still stands on those famous terraces today, the only difference now is the seating in the upper tiers. Swansea City has an equally fierce support, built on years of frustration and, at times, hope. Their supporters like Cardiff's are proud and passionate and long for the success of yesteryear. In the north they can perhaps smile a bit, Wrexham are in the Second Division at the moment. But how much longer will their supporters watch the yearly flirt with promotion before it all gets too boring and Bryan Flynn takes up a better offer? I, for one, hope that all three can do something in the future to cheer us all up.

This book at times reflects the frustration of supporters of Swansea, Cardiff and Wrexham, and at others displays their blatant acts of joy. Memories – the rivalry, the passion, the hope and the frustration are all here, and from those who have watched their clubs for many, many years. You can argue that the buck now stops with the 'big three' from Wales. I, for one, disagree. Our neighbours from Hereford and Chester have shared in the heartache that Wales has to offer, so much so that Hereford United were, not so long ago, Welsh Cup Winners. Yes, in the last ten years Hereford have won the Welsh Cup! The fact that as an English club they couldn't play in Europe mattered not to the supporters of the Bulls, they had won a cup, that's all that mattered to them. They entered the competition knowing that if they won it they would not enter European competition. But all credit to them, they still entered and they won it. And oh, how their supporters loved that. Chester City have the honour of having half their ground in Wales, they couldn't be ignored either. Many a local derby has been fought out at their place with rivals Wrexham. Their supporters are as passionate as any when it comes to the big one with the Robins. You can read about that in this book as well.

The fiercest of rivalries in the British game is documented in these pages, too – Swansea City and Cardiff City. These clubs have fought out many Welsh Cup and English League battles on their pitches. Going back to the turn of the century, teams from these two cities have pitched themselves against one another for the glory of South Wales, be it at football or rugby. Even a game of cricket between these two sets of supporters, before a Wales game in the Eastern bloc eight years ago, deteriorated into a mass brawl, much to the bemusement of the local police. Even now, Glamorgan's cricket games, home and away, suffer as a result of this outrageous rivalry. I have never seen it equalled in my time of watching British football, not even at 'old firm' matches in Glasgow. If you don't know too much of this local hostility, you should have a better idea at the conclusion to this book. I don't expect you to understand it, I still can't, but it happens and it is happening every day in the playgrounds, in the pubs, in the offices and on the factory floor. Where it matters – with the fans.

So how can the supporters have so much passion when their clubs seem to have not a hope when it comes to the world's biggest game? For twenty-five years I have wondered why, and my only conclusion can be that that's what it's all about. Isn't that the attraction for the thousands who still go to these clubs every week? They could go to Chelsea, Arsenal or even Aston Villa, but they don't. Like all real football fans the world over, they wouldn't dare go to another club and try and jump on the bandwagon of success as the trendy bunch have done in the past few years. No, not the real football fan, God forbid. I admit that I have visited other grounds, but I couldn't even get excited at a 5-0 win for Villa, it seemed so foreign to me. I felt alienated. I enjoyed it, but it just wasn't the same as standing on the North Bank at Swansea. You know what I mean, don't you? The Villa fans around me would feel the same if they went to Derby or Liverpool, there is no way they could come to terms with the change in surroundings or the currency in pies or hot drinks. A one night stand maybe, but not a marriage, not even one of convenience, like Zoë's or whoever.

Football is the world game, no matter which team you follow, but the roots of the game are where it is really at. The hard-core loon, and I don't mean thugs, can be found on all the terraces that have deteriorated from years of abuse and lack of care. The anorak and the anorak-tic, the fat, ugly bloke and his son, the highly-paid businessman and the unemployed, the season ticket holder and the student discount card holder, all tread where most care not to. Wales has them all, as much as, if not more than, anywhere else. They have their cross to bear. Since 1958, Pelé and the 1-0 defeat, this nation has had nothing to cheer internationally and only brief flirtations with success at club level – Cardiff in Europe, Swansea in what is now the Premiership and, of course, winning a nondescript trophy at Wembley, and Wrexham will always be Wrexham. Their FA Cup runs recently have been an inspiration to all clubs and their supporters.

Giggsy, you can moan, mate. You can say what you like, but you just haven't got a clue. Freezing your todders off watching our lot is where it's at, believe me. Wales has not had the success it craves because its population is that of Birmingham, that's putting it into context. Unlike the international players we long to bring us success, we don't pick and choose because there is something better on offer. We go because we care, we go because we have to, we go because we go. We go because our country needs us, this country fit for heroes.

Chapter 2

Twenty-Seven Years in a Black and White Scarf

Jonathan Taylor

"A story which starts at Oldham Athletic and swirls towards the Vetch Field, Swansea. Life will never be the same again."

Oldham Athletic. Boundary Park on a cold, wet, windy and (believe it or not) occasionally snowy afternoon in March 1970. Strange as it may seem, this is where my lifetime allegiance to all things Swansea City began. I think I'd better explain, even though I'm not sure I fully understand it myself Let's face it, rational people do not spend twenty-seven years of their life contemplating going to places like Hull for the purposes of getting cold, soaked, abused, and intermittently entertained. Do they?

It's my dad's fault. If there is truly blame to be apportioned, then it rests firmly upon his shoulders. You see, he's English. This is the first of several confessions that I will make during this tale, and all of them will be more devastating than this, because my father didn't ask to be English. He's lived far longer in Wales than he ever did in his home country, and considers himself Welsh, but by an accident of birth he was an Oldham Athletic supporter in his youth. So, in my formative years, whilst my exposure to football was limited to watching 'Match of the Day', I was regaled with tales of the legendary George Hardwick, former player/manager at Oldham. (The irony here is that by the time the moustachioed Hardwick took the Latics to the Third Division North title in 1953, my father had moved south with the RAF during the 1950-51 season.)

We lived (my parents still do) in Llanelli, about 12 miles west of Swansea, but it was during a visit to my father's family in Middleton that I was offered my first real football. Down the road in Manchester, United were playing City, but we had no hope of getting in. So my dad, my Uncle Ernie and I went in the opposite direction, both in terms of geography and League status, to the ramshackle ground that was Boundary Park. It was a Fourth Division match (yes, children, there was a Fourth Division) against Chester, and the Latics won 5-0, an ageing, balding centre-forward named Jim Fryatt getting four of them. I was hooked! No drug on Earth could ever prove to be more addictive, or end up using up so much of my hard-earned cash.

Back home in Wales, I demanded more, and the nearest League club was Swansea Town. The die was cast: there was something homely about Vetch Field, some indefinable quality that just made me feel that this was where I belonged, and that this was where I would watch most of my football. A Welsh Cup clash with Cardiff on May 2nd 1970 ended in defeat, 0-2 (Brian Clark and Peter King), and although I wasn't truly aware of the rivalry between the two sides be-

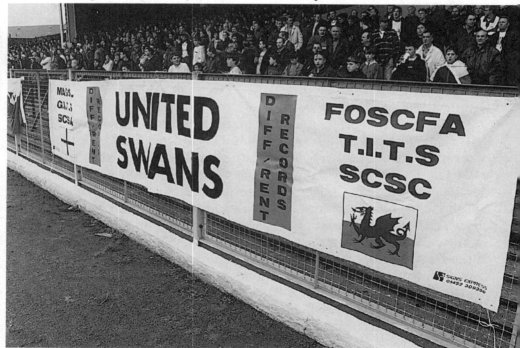

Fan Power hits the Vetch Field: something many would do well not to forget.

fore the game, I certainly was after it. This, however, was followed by a 5-0 thrashing of Shrewsbury Town in September of that year, a result afforded a place in my heart because of a thirty-yard thunderbolt from Lenny Allchurch. By this time, a black-and-white scarf adorned my neck, and the ridicule of my peers at school was something I accepted as par for the course. This was, after all, Llanelli, one of the homes of Welsh rugby, so supporting a football team was bad enough, let alone the fact that that football team wasn't Manchester United. Although I confess (number two, readers!) to having an adolescent fling with Charlton, Law and Best, my school notebooks tended to be adorned with Williams, Thomas and Gwyther.

Before I go any further, I have a third confession to make: I do not recall every match I have ever seen at the Vetch. Memory can be a very strange thing; at times, unnervingly accurate, at others..well, a complete liar. I have programmes in my collection from matches which I certainly attended, but of which I have absolutely no recollection at all. I will, therefore, endeavour throughout this canter through my past to be as accurate and as honest as possible, but I reserve the right to err on some details, and to forget certain players and matches altogether. Psychoanalysis would probably reveal that my mind has blotted out some of the deeper horrors associated with a lifetime at the Vetch.

Horror didn't feature in those early days, though. I was young, innocent, and naive enough to believe that see-sawing between Divisions Three and Four was what football was all about, and I counted myself fortunate to be able go every other Saturday to watch the newly-christened Swansea City struggle through the early Seventies. As far as I was concerned, Roy Bentley was the manager, and that was that: whatever decisions he made about team selection, signing players, tactics and the general running of the club were OK with me. After all, he was the boss, and I was a mere paying schoolboy, not entitled to an opinion because I clearly couldn't see the team playing the way that he saw it – quite often, they were two different games. The reality, of course, was that we had an average team with one or two quality players, but as far as the teenaged Taylor was concerned, these men were icons, small gods who blessed us with their earthly presence once every two weeks. Seems extremely silly now, but, as I said, I'm being honest. Tales of Allchurch (the one that wasn't

Lenny), Dwyer, Medwin et al told by the more senior supporters on the North Bank were all very well, but they didn't mean much to those of us who hadn't had the chance to see them play. If we had, the likes of Carl Slee and the Screen brothers may not have seemed so divine. Still, I paid my pocket money and began to dream of seeing the Swans walk out on to that verdant Wembley turf, one fine Saturday afternoon in the future..

A lot has been written (by better authors than I) about football as part of a young man's rites of passage. So if any of what I will go on to say sounds familiar, either I have subconsciously stolen from others' work, or, more likely, it is a truism that football is a common bond shared by generation upon generation of young boys (and, hopefully, an increasing proportion of young women), and that many thousands of us have gone through similar experiences with different clubs during the burgeoning of our adulthood. At Swansea, my life underwent a sea change when, in 1974, Harry Gregg succeeded Bentley as manager, and for the first time in my brief life, I came to know failure, abject misery and resentment.

In a way, Harry Gregg's team opened Pandora's box for me. I will not name names in order to protect the useless, but suffice to say that the only good facet of Gregg's time at Swansea was his connection with Manchester United that led to the signing of goalkeeper Jimmy Rimmer on loan. However, ineptitude on the park was rapidly followed by the ultimate sin: Gregg replaced the profile of a black swan on the left breast of the Swansea shirt with a red dragon. This, in itself, may not seem like much to the uninitiated, or, indeed, the English amongst you. To me, at that time, it was akin to treason. Yes, granted, we were indubitably a Welsh club, but we weren't the national side, we were the Swans, and as such our strip should reflect our pride in that nomenclature. Gregg's days were clearly numbered, and so was my naivety. This was serious stuff, no longer a pleasant thing to do on Saturday afternoons. I began attending a lot more evening matches, in the belief that if I were there, I could make a difference to the result. Just one more voice added to the North Bank chorus would maybe swing the game in our favour.

Which brings me neatly to my next confession: I still believe that I can make that difference. I'm approaching the age of forty now, and feel I've had sufficient experience of life's vagaries to be able to differentiate between the real and the extremely-bloody-unlikely, but as recently as a couple of years ago, with the Swans' form dipping frighteningly, the recent nightmare of a 0-4 reverse at Lincoln City fresh in mind, and the possibility of dropping out of the play-off places just three matches from the end of the season, I found myself getting in my car and heading for the home game with Mansfield. I did this in the sure and certain belief that, by simply being there, by merely turning up and entering through my usual turnstile to take my customary place upon the North Bank, I would affect the result. You may scoff, ridicule me if you will, but read on. Just after half-time, Mansfield broke away (again) to take a 2-1 lead, and on balance they just about deserved it. Indeed, the neutral supporter (if there is such a creature, but that's another article altogether) would have said that a third Stags' strike was on the cards. They would have said so, however, forgetting that Taylor had come down to stand upon the Bank. His presence obviously had something to do with the fact that substitute Carl Heggs, a man not renowned for any free-scoring exploits since his arrival at the Vetch a couple of seasons ago, scored two of the best goals I've seen at the Vetch in a long time. His second being a lethal first-time volley off his less-favoured left foot to secure a 3-2 Swans victory.

But I digress. Recollecting the Gregg stewardship of Swansea City Football Club often results in such fond diversions, possibly to escape from recollecting said stewardship.

For me, it was the instalment of club stalwart Harry Griffiths as Gregg's replacement that signposted the way to the future. I remember feeling very positive about his appointment; here was a genuine, dyed in the wool, Swansea City man, one whom I believed could make things happen. By the time John Toshack arrived, Harry's foundations had been laid, and the club were well and truly on their way to promotion from the Fourth Division. The tragedy, of course, is that Harry didn't live to see us promoted, but I, and several thousand others, felt his presence at the Vetch that Saturday. Toshack took the plaudits, but Harry took the credit. The king was dead..long live the king!

My destiny now took me to college, and although Pontypridd really isn't that far from Swansea, when you don't have a car and are surviving on a meagre student grant, it became, in local vernacular, a 'tidy distance'. That bugger irony enters the tale again at this point, as between those college years of 1976-79, whilst I was in temporary exile arranging my lifestyle around gigs, pubs, reckless stunts and sometimes the odd lecture or two, the Swans started playing some quality football.

The first promotion was rapidly followed by another, City departing the Third Division with barely a glance over their shoulders. This was staggering stuff. Remember, I'd grown up with the concept of promotion being inevitably succeeded by immediate relegation. A second successive elevation to higher status had roughly the same effect as being told that Newton had it wrong and that gravity no longer applied. And there was I, in absentia, while Johnny Toshack's black-and-white army began their epic rewrite of the Swansea City script.

Confession time again. Whilst at the Polytechnic of Wales, I darkened the doors of Ninian Park on several occasions during Cardiff City's FA Cup run of 1976-77. I am not ashamed to admit this as I went with the express and somewhat less than noble purpose of being witness to the Bluebirds being stuffed silly, but in January they managed a 3-2 victory over Wrexham in a really cracking game of football. I had to wait until the February home tie with Everton in the next round for their eventual come-uppance. I can legitimately lay claim to being probably one of the few Jacks in Christendom to have stood on the old, covered Grange End, when it was still the home of the Cardiff faithful, and not been involved in any head-kicking-in activities. This was because the only place my mates and I could get tickets for the Everton game was the Grange End, so I opted for toughing it out and pretending that I was mute. It worked, and I was rewarded with the sight of Duncan McKenzie beating Albert Larmour on the edge of the box, holding the ball up until Larmour got up off his backside, and then beating him again before scoring. The chain-smoking little lad with the knuckledusters who walked past me at this point did not look at all amused.

Meanwhile, down at Swansea, Toshack was rejuvenated, bending in thirty-yard free-kicks (ask the Exeter City defence) and generally coaxing great performances out of well-meaning but average players. Cue the arrival from Liverpool of no less a talent than Ian Callaghan, come to Swansea to dazzle us with his speed of thought and elegant passing before the sun set on his glittering career. From the same source, by way of contrast, the splendidly uncompromising figure of Tommy Smith came to alarm us with his brutal interpretation of the word 'tackle', and probably looking to upend the sun before it got anywhere near his career.

The League Cup (yes, the League Cup, not the Milk Cup, Coca-Cola Cup, or the Tizer-bloody-trophy) always used to hold more attraction for me than the FA Cup. This may sound strange, but as a Swans fan, I always felt that Mr Hardaker's competition afforded the likes of us more of a realistic tilt at Wembley than its more illustrious older brother did. My definition of 'a realistic tilt' has had to be revised somewhat over the years, and I now freely admit that, with regard to City's aspirations, the words 'slim' and 'chance' spring unbidden to mind.

In 1978, however, the League Cup draw compelled the might of Tottenham Hotspur to consult its map and find its way down to Vetch Field. Spurs manager Keith Burkinshaw had just pulled off the audacious signing of the two Argentineans, Ardiles and Villa, and this at a time when overseas signings were few and far between in the British game. Villa raised a few eyebrows, but we'd all heard of and seen Ardiles because of Argentina's World Cup exploits. The Vetch was so crowded that I simply couldn't struggle through the throng (most of them probably wondering why there weren't any armchairs on the North Bank) to my usual spot, and the atmosphere was electric. Personally, I remember feeling both excited and scared. Excited at the prospect of seeing players of genuine ability and world-class pedigree, and yet scared that these selfsame players would take the Swans to the cleaners. I needn't have worried.

Within thirty seconds of the kick-off, one of the great apocryphal moments in Swansea City's history occurred. Ask anyone at the Vetch these days and they'll tell you they were there, it's one of those moments. As I said, mere moments after the referee blew his whistle for the start of the fray, Ardiles received the ball. Smith, clearly a man with a mission, steams through the midfield towards him, and before the elegant Ardiles can release so much as a short square ball, he is hoisted bodily into the air by one of the worst excuses for a challenge I've ever witnessed. The ref stops play, Smith accepts the customary caution with his customary glower, and Ardiles is nursed back to consciousness by the Spurs physio. In terms of 'the beautiful game', this was a moment of devastating ugliness, but it was extremely effective. Ardiles shrank in stature as the game wore on, visibly reluctant to get involved in anything that might lead to another confrontation with the madman who had tried to kill him in the game's infancy. These days, time has rounded the edges somewhat, and I recall it with a certain hilarity. Ossie Ardiles probably still wakes up screaming. The match finished 2-2, and the replay at White Hart Lane yielded one of the great results in the Swans' history as Tottenham capitulated and City won 3-1.

Ardiles, of course, returned briefly to the Vetch in October 1982, whilst on loan to Paris St Germain during the Falklands War. He had a subdued game, even though Smith was by this time pontificating about football in the Liverpool press, in a way that only ageing ex-footballers can, 'When I was playing..' I am aware, writing this, that there is also a way of writing and talking about the game that only ageing supporters use: I tend to talk about Herbie Williams the way that the previous generation of Swansea support would talk about Ivor Allchurch, and the past is nearly always rose-tinted, especially when, as I mentioned earlier, I cannot recall all the details. And I challenge any veteran Swans' fans to deny that they have ever uttered the words, 'I was there when..'

In any tally of one's life, the worthwhile episodes are almost inevitably going to be counterweighted by those times tinged with the deepest regret. And so to my most painful confession, one which I do not hesitate to make, yet one with which I have possibly never truly come to terms. **I was not at Preston**. At the climax of the Toshack-inspired promotion season of '80 – '81, at approximately 4.45pm on Saturday, May 2nd, I was stood in front of the Radio Rentals showroom in Cheltenham, silently praying (not bad for a complete atheist) that we'd beaten Preston to gain access to the First Division for the first time in the club's history. Although it was impossible to hear sound through the shop window, I knew the Swans had done it when I saw the grinning face of Wyndham Evans fill the screen. I knew that 'Grandstand' wouldn't normally accommodate the likes of Wyndham unless something cataclysmic had taken place.

Why didn't I go? Good question, and one that I have never really explained to myself, let alone anyone else. I'd travelled down to the Vetch for the previous Tuesday's crucial encounter with Luton, at which a win would have been enough to take us up. I'd suffered (yes, suffered is the right word) through the surrender of a two-goal half-time advantage to watch Luton fight back to 2-2, and leave City with the task of going to relegation-threatened Preston needing a win to edge out Howard Kendall's Blackburn Rovers for third place. It didn't matter that Luton's Ricky Hill produced a second-half performance of genuine class to take the game by the scruff of the neck and inspire their comeback. It is with a sense of regret that I look back on several such performances from gifted individuals over the years, aware that I truly did not appreciate them fully at the time – I was too busy suffering for Swansea City.

I had this very conversation in a pub on the way to Scunthorpe! (Why was I going to Scunthorpe? Guess.) My friend and fellow-supporter put forward the point that, despite an obvious love of football and all things Swansea City, he rarely enjoys matches. The Swans' performance and result assumes such importance on the day that actual enjoyment of the footballing fare on offer is usually beyond him. His words struck several resounding chords within me, and make me wonder if the rest of my footballing days will be spent agonising instead of appreciating.

But back to Preston North End, or rather, some way south of there. This was another of those occasions, like the Spurs tie, when people will tell you that they were there. I am honest enough not to try and spin that yarn, even though everyone I have since met and spoken to about the game was so hopelessly drunk on the day that I could quite easily have woven a tangled web of lies to establish my presence in the away end that day. There is very little more to add on this subject, other than to speculate that the only person on the planet possibly more pissed off than me about the whole thing is Nobby Stiles. It cost me some angst-ridden days; it cost Nobby his job.

That initial season in the First Division now seems like some fondly-remembered holiday I once took and I look back on the programmes as I would holiday snaps – and maybe that's quite close to the truth of what happened. A small club went on an outing to the big time, enjoyed itself for a brief while, and then went home. Except that that version of the truth denies the quality of football that Swansea City played against the likes of Manchester United, Liverpool, Spurs, and Leeds, and pays scant attention to the fact that, with six games to go, the Swans were top of the League. In true Swans' fashion, we had a bad patch late on and won only one of those six, finishing sixth, but nevertheless, we had made our mark, and written the club's name in the history books. Irony gets its ugly head to the ball again here, as the draw for the third round of the FA Cup paired us with none other than Liverpool, during a season when we were playing them twice in the League. You wait for years for a fixture with Liverpool, then three come along at once!

The nightmare that followed that season doesn't bear dwelling upon, so I won't, other than to apologise to Ray Kennedy, even though he probably has no idea just how vitriolic my dad and I got regarding his seemingly disinterested, lethargic performances for us. I gave him some serious abuse, which I now regret. I have only two highlights from that season: Ian Walsh scoring twice to beat Manchester City at the Vetch, thus allowing me, at the age of 26, to flash a 'V' at the two old duffers behind me who had spent the whole game (up until he scored his second) giving him some serious verbal abuse; and the 2-1 victory over a strong Aston Villa side, with the young Colin Pascoe turning on a sixpence in the box to volley the winner.

Relegation had become a relative stranger at the Vetch throughout the late seventies and early eighties, no sign of it for quite some time. However, in 1983-84 the bugger bought a season ticket to the Vetch, and seemed to be at most of the away matches, too. I prefer not to re-call too much about our slide back down the divisions, it felt like being in a lift with the 'down' button stuck in position. Suffice to say that I confess to losing the faith after a mind-numbingly awful 0-2 re-verse at Newport County on Saturday, 13th October 1984. The then manager, Colin Appleton, had built a ragbag team of old lags (Tony Kellow, Paul Richardson), fading players (Nigel Stevenson, Chris Ma-rustik), and youngsters being asked to perform beyond their tender years (Colin Pascoe. Dean Saunders). Newport duly turned us over, pausing only to enable both Richardson and Dudley Lewis to get sent off for throwing a punch and 'foul and abusive language' respectively. It was dismal, and as I left Somerton Park, I not only had to cope with my despair and anger at yet another abject defeat, I also found myself dodging the 'visiting' Cardiff City psychopaths, determined to give their club a bad name. The whole sorry experience left me in a very reflective mood, and on the train during the journey home, I came to the conclusion that I just couldn't take this any more. Life was hard enough as it was, without Swansea City dragging me down with them week after week. There must be better things to do with my life, mustn't there?

And so it was that I found myself visiting a family friend for dinner in Cheltenham on the evening that the Swans (now under John Bond, Appleton's Vetch career having lasted just six unfortunate months) faced Bristol City in the last match of the 1984-85 season, and needed just a draw to avoid the trapdoor to the Fourth Division opening beneath them. I had been away for the best part of that season, observing the descent from afar. I told myself that American football on Channel 4 was more fun, all the while avoiding the basic truth that because the Chicago Bears really meant very little to me, it didn't hurt when they lost. Anyway, back to that dinner invitation. I wasn't a vegetarian then, and I vividly recall not only the lamb chops and ratatouille, but also a sudden burning desire at 9.15pm to get to the television set. I needed to see that result, and the palpable relief when I saw the 0-0 scoreline on the screen made me realise that my estrangement from Swansea City was over.

By this time I was working shifts, so my return to the fold was hampered by unsocial hours. Working two weekends out of every three made it bloody difficult to follow your team, and if I managed five or six games a season I counted myself lucky. Having said that, the Swans, after luring me back with the possibility of having put the brakes on the runaway return to Division Four, promptly hit the accelerator, and there were some matches that I was glad to have missed. The low point was achieved at Molineux in March 1987. An injury crisis had forced Terry Yorath out of retirement and the manager's seat in the dugout, and back into a sweeper role. He was crap, so were the rest of the team, and our forward pairing of Love and McCarthy was outshone by a young Wolves duo named Mutch and Bull. There was snow on the terracing, the West Midlands police were unpleasant to say the least, and 0-4 flattered the Swans. But though disappointed, I was at peace with myself – I knew exactly why I was there. Football wasn't just a game, it was an escape from the mundanities of life, from the 6am alarm ringing, from the bus being late, from the cost of my shopping rising, from standing in the queue at the post office, from..well, just about everything.

Back then, I always used to think that I was alone: a Swansea supporter in Gloucestershire. Then, through the auspices of the late and much lamented Swans fanzine *Jackmail*, I met a bloke called Keith. Within a matter of months we were on our way to Leyton Orient with another bloke called Dave, and now, some five years later, we're the Midlands Avon Gloucester Swans. And there are scores of us, dotted all over the country (the MAGS title having become something of a misnomer these days). Our third annual end-of-season dinner was attended by 60-plus folk, with Steve Jones and no less a light than player-manager Jan Molby in attendance. Thus, football at Swansea continues to provide for me what it has always done, in varying ways: companionship, and the knowledge that no matter what our different backgrounds, occupations, beliefs, values and attitudes may be, everybody on the minibus on a Saturday shares the One True Faith.

This faith was finally rewarded at Wembley Stadium, on the pleasant, sunny afternoon of April 24th 1994, when that boyhood dream of mine came true. As Torpey struck home the deciding penalty, I knew exactly why I've stuck by Swansea City for all these years. OK, it wasn't the FA Cup, it was the Autoglass Trophy Final, but nevertheless there I was, watching my team win something. And right at that moment when club captain John Cornforth lifted the trophy, I was as happy as I've ever been.

In a time even before Stanley Matthews, Duncan Edwards, and very baggy shorts, the poet Wordsworth (culturally, about as far removed from Tommy Smith as you get) was an advocate of communing with nature, of getting what your soul needed from finding a leafy glade and quietly writing rural, pantheistic verse. Sounds very pleasant, but let's be honest, shall we? Where's the anticipation? The excitement? The emotional highs and lows? The adrenaline rush? I confess (my final confession, readers) that I enjoy great works of verse, but in terms of an overview of times, places, people, and events in my life, it's a latest score of Poetry 0, Football 1. It's difficult to explain, but I still experience a unique feeling, an intense moment, that occurs around 3 o'clock every Saturday afternoon. In those seconds just before the referee blows his whistle, regardless of the size of the crowd, the quality of the opposition, or the team's recent fortunes, anything is possible. Even at the Vetch.

Not only had the Swans made it to Wembley . . .they went on to win!

Chapter 3

Bordering on Insanity
Colin Mansley

"Chester City is a Welsh club, isn't it?"

The Golden Years

What's an account of Chester City Football Club doing in a book about Welsh football? You may well ask. City fans regularly assert their Englishness in matches with Welsh opposition – yet the truth, unpalatable though it may seem to many City faithful, is that it is actually possible to be Welsh **and** support Chester.

The ancient city is very close to the border with Wales and presides over a river more Welsh than English. The River Dee has been a fickle friend to Chester over the years. A couple of centuries ago it left the city in the lurch commercially as it started to silt up, allowing the little fishing village of Liverpool to grow in relative importance as a port. Just think, if it weren't for this tiny accident of historical geography, it would be Chester which now boasted two teams in the Premiership.

The Dee has also shifted its course a few times and has left the border with Wales behind. This second accident of historical geography has proved acutely embarrassing to the club's authorities and fans since the building of the Deva Stadium in 1992. The new ground is sited on land reclaimed from the river and, in fact, straddles its old course, and with it the boundary between England and Wales. When it was discovered that the original plan for the stadium meant that the main stand and club offices would be on the Welsh side of this arbitrary line, the plan was hastily redrawn. Now the main stand at the Deva looks across to Hope Mountain and the Clwydian range and City fans are often dazzled, less by the brilliance of Chester's football, than by the sun as it sets over the foothills. All in the cause of being able to say the Chester is an English club. The official line is that the offices, main stand and dressing rooms are in England, whilst as soon as the players run on to the pitch they are playing in Wales.

This was, at the time, more than an exercise in academic nationalism. The secretary of the Welsh FA, a certain Mr Alun Evans, had made claims on Chester becoming a Welsh club. He had issued a draconian edict that all Welsh clubs must play in the League of Wales in order to qualify for European competition. As this would have involved clubs like Swansea and Cardiff playing Porthmadog, Connah's Quay Nomads and Llansantffraid on a regular basis, the former slumbering giants, fearing for their gate revenue, politely declined. Colwyn Bay still harboured ambitions of working their way up the English pyramid system of the lower leagues, and went into enforced exile rather than play in the Welsh League.

Chester did not want to get sucked into Evans' plans for a league of total obscurity and dubious quality, and continue to draw the line just in front of the main stand. But Evans is a pretty dogged character,

Chester City's new ground, "The Deva Stadium": half Welsh, half English. The location became a thorn in the club's side.

however, and has made sarcastic remarks about no club having their basis of operation in the club car park (the only part of the Deva Stadium that can categorically be said to be in England). What will happen when he finds out that the club has to apply to the Welsh authorities for the licence to sell alcohol in the directors' lounge?

As not even Swansea and Cardiff have any desire to ply their trade in the League of Wales, no amount of technical argument is ever likely to get Chester in. As for crossing the border to play Wrexham, well that's another matter entirely. It's the only international local derby match in the entire Football League. Chester fans have been proud to fly the flag for England at this fixture for over sixty-five years. It's just a pity that those selected to represent the national team haven't always had Chester's best interests at heart. One shameful day in May 1980, Ron Greenwood led the national side (containing such stars as Hoddle and Brooking) to the Racecourse Ground, only to be thrashed 4-1 by the Welsh (managed by Mike **England**). The gleeful locals, showing a modicum of wit at a level higher than one would normally expect, began singing to the hapless English, 'Are you Chester in disguise?' No way would we have capitulated so spinelessly.

Yet another irony in this history of border rivalry is that the twelve miles of countryside between Chester and Wrexham is a very English-looking part of Wales. Wrexham's parish church would not look out of place in Somerset or the Cotswolds. Even the name 'Wrexham' is one of Saxon origin, which the latter-day Welsh spelling of 'Wrecsam' can't disguise. So a simplistic Welsh/English rivalry can only be skin deep. For if Chester (the 'City' was added in 1983) are an English club, then more than their fair share of star players have been Welsh. The present manager, Kevin Ratcliffe, was a stalwart defender for the Welsh national side. His schoolmate, Ian Rush, was Chester's most famous export to Liverpool, and again hailed from across the border. Going back further, Ron Davies, one of the best headers of the ball in living memory, and Ian Edwards both had their main chance with Chester and went on to Welsh international honours. The first time I saw Edwards play while he was with Chester was in the Welsh Under 21 side, against Scotland at Easter Road. The most capped player while on Chester's books is still Bill Lewis, who won seven caps with Wales.

Until 1980 (when they lost in the fifth round to Merthyr Tydfil, the only goalscorer a certain Pratt), Chester, along with other English sides such as Shrewsbury, Hereford and Kidderminster, used to enter the Welsh Cup. They won it three times – in 1908, 1933 and 1947. On two occasions they secured the trophy at Wrexham's ground, but their opponents were Connah's Quay and Merthyr Tydfil. In 1933, however, the Welsh Cup was won on English soil as 15 000 turned up in the pouring rain to see Chester overcome their nearest and dearest rivals.

Before the game, the band of the Royal Welsh Fusiliers paraded, complete with regimental goat – and Chester fans' derisory name for all things Wrexham is 'The Goats' to this day. The Chester captain, rejoicing in the name of Baden Herod, won the toss and – like his Biblical namesake – he and his followers showed no mercy to their opponents. Although played on a quagmire, the standard of play was reported to have been excellent. The FAW Secretary, Ted Robbins, had been at Wembley for the FA Cup Final between Everton and Manchester City a few days before and thought it had been nothing like as good a game as the one he had seen for the Welsh Cup that night.

Those were the glory times for Chester at their old home ground, imaginatively named The Stadium. Most of us knew it as Sealand Road, where the home end was situated – the name itself indicative of the area's origin on the plain left behind by the Dee's meanderings. Now that same sacred site is desecrated by an out-of-town retail park and the City faithful have to battle their way through traffic jams of people queuing to purchase consumer durables. The name of City's new ground – Deva – refers to Chester's Roman origins, a rough translation being 'stadium of the gods'. Most of the local population, however, remember 'The Deva' as being the name of the City's residential institute for people with mental health difficulties or, as our more robust forbears at the turn of the century called it, The County Lunatic Asylum. The new football ground is an even more out-of-town development – so far out its nearest neighbours are the cattle market and derelict abattoir and, just across Bumpers Lane, the household waste disposal site. And, of course, it straddles that Anglo-Welsh dividing line.

Siege and Exile

What did Chester's football club do to deserve banishment to such a desolate place? Answer: they had the audacity to own their own ground, a tempting little piece of real estate, ripe for a bit of cherry picking. Slowly but surely through the 1970s and 80s, the retail outlets sprang up around The Stadium like the encroaching woods of Dunsinane and proved just as menacing. First, it was Texas Homecare along Stadium Way, then Kwiksave across Sealand Road. The club itself realised some of its assets and sold the training ground for development by Slough Estates. MFI popped up next to Kwiksave, and when the neighbouring greyhound stadium was demolished to make way for a Halford's Superstore, the premier site for football in Chester was all but surrounded.

Chairman Eric Barnes had mooted plans for relocating in the early 1980s, but any development of the Sealand Road site was blocked by the City Council until the football club agreed to pay for a new relief road, thus removing all possible financial gain from a move. When the club was faced with a winding-up order in 1986, in moved property firm BCH, who paid off £138 000 of City's debts and gained a controlling interest in the club. The stalemate with the City Council planning department persisted – though City fans were underwhelmed by a proposal to build a new ground just over the Welsh border – and so, in November 1989, the club (lock, stock and barrel-chested centre forward) was put up for sale. Even worse, the club's owners offered vacant possession of Sealand Road from May 1990.

On 28 April, City fans turned up to Sealand Road hoping that Chester would secure their place in the Third Division the following season. This they duly did by beating Rotherham 2-0. But where they would be playing their home matches remained a mystery. The Scottish construction company Morrison (not to be confused with the supermarket chain of that name) had bought the club and insisted that Sealand Road must be vacated. But the efforts of Chairman Barnes to find a home for our football had proved fruitless. He had presided over Chester's addition of 'City' to their title in 1983 – perhaps a more fitting title would have been 'Wanderers'. Any way, he resigned a few days before the Rotherham match. Most fans assumed he had been paid his thirty pieces of silver by Morrison (why else would graffiti at The Stadium proclaim him synonymous with the twelfth disciple?). In fact, he and BCH were later to sue the club and take it to the brink of extinction.

Barnes, who had Manchester City connections, had previously explored the possibility of Chester sharing Maine Road while a new ground was built. Peter Swales would have none of it. (Ironically, in 1996 the present chairman tried, as part of a consortium, to buy out Manchester City and use Chester as a feeder club.) Approaches were made by Morrison to Warrington and then Widnes, the Rugby League clubs twelve miles along the M56 – but they, too, were unwilling to have Chester as lodgers. Fans' sensibilities were severely tested when it was announced that a ground-share with Wrexham had been agreed. Supporters of thirty and forty years' standing vowed they would never go **there** to watch City play – it was unthinkable! Just as the unthinkable was about to become awful reality, it was the North Walian police who ruled it out. Although Chester fans have never been so grateful to such an unlikely body as the Welsh constabulary, they still had nowhere to hang their hats for the following season.

Things were beginning to get desperate, with the Football League doubting the likelihood of Chester being able to fulfil their fixtures. Barnet, then a non-league club, were, it was rumoured, put on stand-by should Chester fail to find a home. At the eleventh hour (more like one minute to midnight), a home was found. The good news was that it was in Cheshire; the bad news – about as far away in the county as it was possible to get from Chester. City were to play the next couple of seasons in the far-flung east of Cheshire, at the quaintly named and picturesque Moss Rose ground, Macclesfield. This represented a round trip of eighty miles for Cestrians – not a particularly convenient journey either. The club put on subsidised double-decker buses for 'home' matches, but the tortuous nature of the route to Macc and the somewhat basic suspension system of corporation buses soon meant that this particular method of getting to a match was christened 'the white knuckle ride' (by Chris Courtenay Williams).

So we weren't too happy about Chester playing on or over the Welsh border, but this was taking it to ridiculous extremes. Macclesfield's almost in Yorkshire for heaven's sake. When Chester played Bradford and Huddersfield at home, the away fans had a shorter journey to the match than we did, and as for playing Stockport – we were virtually in their own back yard!

Blooming Moss Rose

The two-year episode in the club's history which followed seems tinged with unreality. I began to wake frequently in the middle of the night from a dream that Chester had been forced to play all their matches in a school gymnasium. Ironically, my home was now in Sale and so my team had moved closer to where I lived – talk about Mohammed and the mountain. So for the next two seasons I enjoyed the short journey from South Manchester to Macclesfield, taking in some of the more magical and mysterious corners of the Cheshire countryside, including Alderley Edge, where legend relates that Merlin wanders in the twilight hours.

The Moss Rose itself, sited on the southern outskirts of Macclesfield, has a picturesque setting. As City used to run out to strains of 'The Big Country', from the popular side, opposite what passes for a grandstand, we lifted our eyes to the splendid views of the Pennine foothills – the stepped outline of Tegg's Nose in the foreground and the distinctive hummock of Shutlingsloe on the horizon. The view is rivalled in the Football League only by the outlook across the Humber estuary from Blundell Park.

Another compensation was that Macclesfield, being a mill town, is replete with pubs of every description. Two of them virtually encroach on the Moss Rose, and appeared to be overwhelmed with visiting supporters on several occasions. With a little more planning and discernment, some rather nice watering holes can be explored within a short distance of the ground. The appropriately named Fool's Nook was one favourite with us. (So, too, was a hotel in a quite plush, rural location, which must remain anonymous due to the threat of discovery by the visiting hordes who will soon be arriving to celebrate Macclesfield's newly achieved League status.) On one occasion, we celebrated a narrow but ecstatic win against Stockport in a nearby village inn. We found ourselves sharing the tiny public bar with residents of the Moss Rose area who were taking refuge from the big match atmosphere. Soon we were reciting the whole sorry tale of how we had come to be in exile as a football club and how the previous chairman had sold us down the river. 'Better be careful what you say,' came the reply, 'this is Eric Barnes's local.'

Chester's former chairman was conspicuous by his absence at their new home. So, too, were the new owners, Morrison, who remained aloof in their Scottish eyrie whilst communicating occasionally with the sole remaining director, Ray Crofts. Also missing from most of City's home matches were about a thousand regulars, which meant that the average attendance plummeted to just over 1500. One fateful night in the Freight Rover cup-tie against Bury, a meagre 409 turned out – this was the lowest of the low. On a number of occasions we suspected that the attendance figures had actually been adjusted **upwards** in order to make them look half-respectable (rather than downwards in order to fiddle the taxman).

The heroic spirit of the remaining Chester fans continued undaunted. One night, in a cup-tie with Preston, I recall about ten of them clustered behind the goal and taunting the visiting Lancastrians with chants of, 'What's it like to see a crowd?' I've always had a soft spot for the self-effacing style of humour (except against Wrexham, of course). And if the crowds were decidedly thin, then there was no problem about getting a good view of the match, or in being able to arrive at the last minute, park the car with relative ease and stroll through the turnstiles.

In any case, parts of the Moss Rose are so cramped that it needed only twenty-five of us to squeeze into the small paddock in front of the main stand and, hey presto, there was all the big-match atmosphere of the Stretford End of twenty years ago! This was certainly the place to be if you wanted entertainment. The two dugouts were so close that you could touch them, and such august personalities as Bobby Gould and Alan Ball had no hiding place from the sarcastic mirth and incisive wit for which Cestrians are famous. No one, though, could compete with City's off-the-wall manager, Harry McNally. He would frequently have those behind him in tears of laughter as he berated players of both sides. If Joe Hinnigan, the physio, spent longer than thirty seconds attending to an injured blue then McNally would bawl, 'Stick a plaster on it.' At the same time he would rage at the player to get on his feet again. Several of the younger players were visibly scared of him – it was rumoured that he had hung an apprentice's shirt on a coat-hanger, then on a coat hook, with the apprentice inside the shirt at the time.

There were more than just rumours attached to the infamous players' Christmas party in 1990, when McNally and Keith Birtschin both ended up in hospital, having submerged their sorrows too liberally in alcohol. Ray Crofts went to visit McNally and, seeing the state he was in, didn't have the heart to sack him. This was eventually proved a wise move as, despite his foibles, McNally's tenacious spirit was the main reason Chester avoided relegation when in exile, with all the odds stacked against them.

In February the following season, when City were turned over 5-2 at the Moss Rose by fellow relegation candidates Darlington, few thought they would preserve their place in the Third Division. Harry was now the subject of verbal abuse from City fans at the end of their tether – though he gave back as good as he got. Still he managed to cajole his charges into a dogfight against the drop. A corner was turned when 871 saw City hammer Exeter (with Alan Ball going Ballistic at the prospect). But they then seemed to have blown it when, against Birmingham, veteran baldy Barry Siddall let an injury time free-kick squirm under his body. Jasper Carrott and his fellow Brummies, who outnumbered Cestrians by about three to one at a supposedly away fixture, would have cheered so loud they could have been heard back home if they hadn't been convulsed with laughter. One final, forlorn-looking chance awaited City at the Victoria Ground, Stoke. There, over 18 000 gathered to see the team from the Potteries clinch promotion. Instead, incredibly, they saw the tigerish Gary Bennett dispossess Noel Blake and fire home the only goal, ten minutes from time. Benno's celebrations were extravagant and outrageous, but were sweet expression of escape from relegation.

Now, it seemed, Chester would be able to return to their home city in triumph – their Third Division status preserved. (In fact, the restructuring caused by the Premiership meant that they actually began at home in Division Two.) At long last, work had begun on the new Deva stadium at the end of January. In their lunch breaks and at other idle moments, City supporters would trek along Bumpers Land and gaze over the hedge to watch work progressing in the farmer's field which straddles the border. We saw a stream being diverted (it tried to reclaim its old course during the Deva's first season!), spindly floodlight pylons being erected, and rather small terraces going up.

The new stadium looked to be little more than Subbuteo deluxe dimensions and, sure enough, despite originally published plans for a ground with capacity just below 10 000, the finished article was a bare League minimum of 6 000. By this time, most Chester fans were just glad to see some sort of home. Quaint and picturesque though the Moss Rose was, it would never be the place to host Chester's long term survival.

Rovers' Return

All the time the lads had been toiling heroically on the slope of Moss Rose, the derelict Sealand Road Stadium had stood, gaunt and thistle-infested, as a reminder of former glories. Its presence rubbed salt into the raw emotional wounds of City fans as the buses transporting them to Macclesfield went past their empty home. Once work had commenced on the new ground, the old came down. Typically, opportunities were missed to preserve any link between the club's history and its future. A terracotta plaque commemorating the subscriptions of supporters towards a section of the ground was scandalously smashed up in the demolition. Now the only hints that Sealand Road was the home of a football club are the old electricity substation with its 'Chester FC' label, and the approach road to Pizza Hut, which has been named 'Old Seals Way', thus preserving a rather embarrassing nickname which the club dropped years ago. My father and I picked our way round the debris one afternoon as we watched Sealand Road being shredded. Two small, brick fragments of the popular side currently adorn a shelf in my bedroom – the only tangible reminder of over twenty years of supporting.

Though we were glad to be back in the old town, the first season back in Chester was anticlimactic in playing terms. Spiritually exhausted by their efforts in exile, City's form slumped. Gary Bennett, who had found himself charged with receiving stolen property, was suddenly persona non grata, and went on a free transfer to Wrexham (though he would often return to sit in the stand at the Deva). A weary McNally was sacked before Christmas. Chester were relegated by a mile. Wrexham (cough, spit) went in the opposite direction.

McNally, who had worked miracles when Chester played in Merlin's country, was replaced by the sorcerer's apprentice, Graham Barrow. Playing a brand of football beautiful to behold, and in a traditional kit of blue and white stripes and black shorts (which the fans had long clamoured for but only Barrow had delivered), City swept straight back up again the following season. But the playing fortunes of the club were not reflected behind the scenes. Morrison were still the owners and had been dragging their feet interminably about selling to local business consortiums. Consequently, there was no money to strengthen the staff after promotion and Barrow quit, to be followed by all but half a dozen of the players. Much to the anger and frustration of the fans, Chester (as with Barnet the season previously) were virtually relegated before the season had begun.

The only consolation in a campaign which saw us yo-yo back to the basement was that in our first League encounters for many years with the old enemy from across the border – we were undefeated. This represented quite a considerable achievement when, on Valentine's Day 1995, no love was lost between us and our rivals as we clashed at the Racecourse. Gary Bennett – who the Wrexham fans had been mightily suspicious of when he first arrived – was now their darling, having scored a sackful of goals for them. Within two minutes of the start of the match he had the ball in the net, but only for his effort to be disallowed. Ten minutes later his penalty was saved by David Felgate, and we began to wonder whether he still had a soft spot for us after all. When, a minute later, Chester were given a penalty, Eddie Bishop coolly rammed the ball in to give us the lead. By half-time City were in tatters, Wrexham having taken a 2-1 advantage – Bennett managing to score legitimately. Even worse, Chester stalwarts Lightfoot and Bishop had been sent off in a crazy sixty seconds before half-time. Bennett had mysteriously fallen in a crumpled heap at Bishop's feet in an off-the-ball incident.

City fans seethed with self-righteous indignation during the interval, then cheered every effort to keep out Wrexham in the second half, bellowing their bile every time the ball went within yards of Bennett. Five minutes from the end of the game, we prepared to give our nine-man team a prolonged standing ovation for keeping the score down to 2-1, despite a predictable onslaught from the home side. Then Andy Milner latched on to a hacked clearance, ran half the length of the pitch and curled the equaliser into the top right-hand corner. All of the clichés in the world could not describe the emotional scenes of celebration that followed. It was the sort of moment that every football fan lives for, and lives off for many years to follow.

So, in the hope of more such magic moments, you will continue to find me standing towards the English end of the home terracing at the Deva Stadium (third crush barrier from the left). After all, when you are close to the border, it is best to know resolutely and unequivocally where you stand – well, probably anyway. Oh, and things might be looking up – Chester signed a new forward for the 1997-8 season, a chap called Gary Bennett from, now where was it again? Er, Wrexham!

Chester City fans en route to Swansea for the 2nd leg of the 1997 Play Offs.

Chapter 4

Swansea, oh Swansea!
The reality of loyalty

Keith Haynes

*A gritty look at Swansea City from the terraces of
the eighties.*

I have followed Swansea City for as long as I can remember, foolishly
or otherwise. It is a labour of love, no matter what happens or how we
play, I will always be there, home or away, it matters not.

Everyone remembers their first football match, it is usually with a
parent, and more often or not it is watching your local team play.
Now, the majority of local teams are going to be of a lower standard
than, say, Man United, Liverpool or a host of London clubs, but as a
five-year-old it matters not. The first time is the making or breaking of
a kid, he or she will either love it or hate it. I loved it and haven't
looked back, until now that is.

Haverfordwest County against Pembroke Borough was my first
game. It was at The Bridge Meadow, Haverfordwest on a freezing cold
day in 1968. I was five years of age. I couldn't tell you the score, what I
can recall is the seemingly massive crowd (at that age, any crowd is
massive) and a goal at the very end of the game, a header that went in
off the post from a comer. The attendances at The Meadow in those
days were around the 2000 mark, which was not bad for a Welsh
League side. However, they had been a dominant force in Welsh
League football, and any loss in form would have seen the gate virtually disappear. Today the Bluebirds (yes – Swans fans can follow a
team with a nickname like this!) pull in crowds of between 300 and
600, and I still go whenever I am home.

That game was my introduction to football, and to a lifelong love
affair that would introduce me to more emotions than any relation-

ship could ever hope to achieve. It would also bring me close to a group of individuals who are the embodiment of what it means to be a true football fan. I hope I do them justice.

Whilst Haverfordwest County were setting the Welsh League alight, Swansea City, their near neighbours, were then a 'Town' and struggling, as ever, to maintain their Football League status. The change to 'City' did nothing to mend the side's pathetic attempts to get out of the rut which was Fourth Division football. 1970 may as well have been 1870, new name, same old story. I saw us lose more times than not during my apprenticeship at the Vetch. I am not a keeper of records, but I would say that from the first twenty games I witnessed at the Vetch I saw the Swans win only once, against Cardiff City, 3-1. I fondly recall David Gwyther and his 'score at all costs' philosophy, and from any part of his anatomy! The funniest goal I saw him score was against Huddersfield at the Vetch, when he 'arsed' it home after the ball came down off the bar. He lunged at the ball backwards with his backside sticking out and the ball flew into the net, again off the bar and via the keeper's face – great stuff! He was my boyhood hero.

As I grew older I became aware of the noise that erupted at times from the Swansea North Bank. I used to stand on the old terracing behind the east goal, but as I grew a bit older I took my rightful place on the North Bank, and joined in the noise that used to sound quite intimidating if you were not a part of it. Well, at the big games anyway, and there were a few – not many, but a few. For some reason, between the ages of 10 and 13 I lost my affection for the team, but not for football. We had moved to London so I transferred myself to Chelsea. A bit of a cop-out maybe, but I always kept one eye on the Swans. Like a concerned investor, I knew that one day I would return.

And return I did, with one John Toshack. It was the happiest coincidence that I have ever known. Now I don't intend to give you a blow-by-blow account of this era of Swansea City, suffice to say we were shit hot, and very few teams could match us on the pitch. It culminated in the famous 1981-82 season, which again is well documented and which will never be matched. We nearly won what is now the Premiership that year, and we did it playing the best football I have ever seen from a Swansea team. To beat Man United, Liverpool, Arsenal and all was a pleasure, and that goal from Gary Stanley against Man City was awesome, absolutely, bloody awesome. We finished sixth that season in May 1982, and I didn't go again until 1985. It wasn't that I gave up on them, it was deeper than that: I had seen all I thought could be seen as a football fan. I also had a career as a musician to pursue, and this took me away for weeks on end. Again I kept one eye on the results, even attended a number of away games, but sadly, for three years I did not even get close to The Vetch Field. (Except, that is, when my band played The Swansea Marina with The UK Subs, and even then it didn't feel the same.)

My return to the fold came in the old Third Division for the opening game of the 1985-86 season. It was against Millwall, away. Now The Den never really intimidated me as a football fan, maybe that was the reason I was a football fan and not a thug of any description. That day was a complete bloody nightmare, and we lost. I travelled up to London with a load of mates from my home town of Haverfordwest, a Swansea stronghold with no trace of a Cardiff fan in those days, well, none that ever made themselves known. We arrived in London at about 11am, which was our first mistake. About 500 Swansea fans had already arrived in the capital and there had been some problems. We were put in the same basket by The Metropolitan Police. We intended to visit a few record shops prior to the game, but instead we were locked in a massive warehouse for two hours, until enough of us were gathered to be escorted to Millwall. One PC (who, coincidentally, I have met since) revelled in his position of power and made a big thing of our heritage. The usual sheep-shaggers thing etc. Having spoken to him since, it seems he learned a lesson that day, as did I.

Being a real fan, I had no problem with wearing my team's colours to games or carrying my trusty flag, little did I realise it would make me a target for one hell of a beating. I don't want to dwell on the problems our game has faced in recent times, that is not what this book is about, but suffice to say all real football fans have a story to tell, and this is mine. By about 2.30pm we had been placed in the then away end at Millwall, and to be honest I was very annoyed with the way we had been treated and humiliated by The Met. From the time I got into the ground to the time I left, I witnessed more intense hatred than I have seen at a game since. The Swansea fans, well alleged fans, were intent on attacking all and sundry and about 200 had managed to get into the Millwall end. It was horrific, the fighting went on for a good twenty minutes and people from both sides were injured. I have never really understood this particular form of entertainment – after all, if you want a good fight why not just pick on the nearest person in your own town centre, why travel 200 miles to do it? Anyway, to cut a long story short, the game ended about 5.15pm and, as I said, we lost. A number of Swansea fans (?) claimed a victory that day on the terraces, but who for? Not for me, it spoiled the whole day out. And even more importantly, not for the Swansea fan who took a bigger hiding than I did, for just being there. He was a regular at Swans' games in those days, a real fan. He was always draped in a Welsh flag with Llanelli Swans proudly embossed on it, and always having a laugh. I knew him as Tropper. He had a vast knowledge of all things Swansea City. He was attacked for being in the wrong place at the wrong time, as I was, and he died later evening. He collapsed at home, he was 17. What price loyalty?

Other absolutely absurd things have happened at Swans' games. An FA Cup replay between the Swans and Crystal Palace, held for whatever reason at Ninean Park, Cardiff, ended in tragedy. Two Swansea fans were killed in an attack outside the ground, one Cardiff fan was never to walk again. Why the hell he was there is a question I have asked many times. What price loyalty? Twenty-three thousand fans attended the game that night, Swansea won, but did they really? The disgusting scenes between Swansea and Cardiff that were witnessed at Ninean Park in 1993 were totally unexplainable and unnecessary. Thousands of pounds worth of damage was caused to the ground that night and for what? The gap between us and our rivals in the capital has never been wider than since that game. Cardiff are still going on about it, possibly because they are not used to such things happening at their own ground. They are more used to seeing it being dished out by their own supporters than being on the receiving end. Another victory? I think not. Writing in this manner must be similar to counselling of some sort, it may not read that well but I feel better for sharing my thoughts with you.

Following my team in the past seven years has bordered on an obsession. We have had some tremendous days out to Wembley in the Autoglass Trophy, and the play-offs. Many games I have attended have been intense affairs – the FA Cup games against Liverpool and Newcastle United, not forgetting beating Middlesboro at their place in 1995. A number of games against Wycombe in the Autoglass Trophy in 1994 were a nightmare to watch, one mistake and our Wembley dream would collapse. It didn't, and we went on to beat Huddersfield at Wembley. It was brilliant beating Cardiff City in the snow at the Vetch in 1995, 4-1 was a pleasure, it should have been IO. For some reason we gave up and seemed to feel sorry for them, how could they? Dave Penney scored a cracker that night. He went on to captain Cardiff City. How could he? He is now at Doncaster Rovers.

I love to see Cardiff lose and revel in their disappointments, although I know that if they were to leave the Football League, Welsh football would never be the same again. And the same would be true if we left. Both of us need to get out of the current turmoil that is the Third Division before the idiots at the Welsh FA get their way and force us into the League of Wales. I read of the plan for Swansea, Cardiff and Wrexham to join this new era of Welsh football. No way will the fans ever let this happen, trust me. The League of Wales is a joke, run by jokers, for joke teams – I think you get the point. European football is the carrot they dangle, I, for one, hope they choke on it. I don't want to jump around all over the place, from season to season, but I thought I had better put a few things to you before I concentrate on the emotional roller coaster I have been on since the age of five.

The season prior to getting into the **then** First Division in 1981 was a nothing affair. We never really looked like getting promotion until the last few weeks. And even then it was close, very close. I have to admit that I thought we had blown it at the last home game of that season, drawing 2-2 with Luton at the Vetch, a game we should have won. The final game of that campaign was a visit to Preston North End, a game we had to win to be assured of promotion. Now I didn't realise just how much this particular game had gripped the population of Wales and, of course, Swansea fans everywhere. Over 10 000 made the trip to Preston that day, again a game which is well documented. We won 3-1, and I will never forget the feeling of elation when Jeremy Charles rammed home the third goal.

My story on that day began at 7am, after a hefty night on the beer with the chaps. We had decided to go by car, five of us and a whole load of lager as fuel. The driver, Dai, had volunteered his services in the pub the night before. We were raring to go – all the usual stuff, scarves flying out of the windows and full of anticipation. To be honest, I never thought we would get there, Preston seemed a thousand miles away. Suffice to say, it was lucky we left as early as we did. It takes a good two hours to get out of Wales if you live down west as we did, and this was not a problem for us. The M50 was soon covered in double-quick time and my anxiety was beginning to go away. Oh, how foolish! Dai became a man possessed. It was either the sight of the MGB GT being driven at considerable speed or the driver, a raven-headed young lady, which turned our Dai from a normal, placid sort into a double-horned devil, mad-beasty chap in a fleeting moment.

The change was astonishing. He upped the speed of the old Avenger and locked in behind her, cruising at 90 mph, for about fifty yards, and then the bottom dropped out of the car. Literally! The gearbox, deciding that Dai was a complete burden, was sending all manner of sparks along the motorway – due to the fact it was dragging along the tarmac. All we saw was a massive hole in the floor of the car. Technically, we were bollocksed. Dai, deciding that he would shed his mad bloke's skin, slowed down, and we trundled along the slow lane at 30 mph, locked in fourth gear. Amazingly, this got us well into Lancashire but took some four hours to achieve, by 2pm we were stranded at a service station ten miles from Preston. There was only one thing for it, we had to join the AA! Now I am sure a lot of you have been in a similar predicament at some time in your driving career, wishing you were a member of some sort of road recovery organisation or other. We were no different. The problem was all of us, with the exception of another Dai, a passenger, were totally skint. Dai 2 was our only hope. He obliged by signing Dai I up for a year's membership with the AA, and was immediately told that any recovery would not take place until 24 hours had passed. We vowed revenge.

In times like this it is every man for himself. Time was cracking on and with some ten miles and a town centre to negotiate, things were looking bleak. The thumbs came out, that is with the exception of Dai the driver, who remained with his car. He waited foolishly, like some hopeless parent, there was no reason for it. On the slip road of the service station, a number of vehicles hooted us as they drove past our forlorn faces. I was getting desperate. Then out of the sunshine drove this god of all motor vehicles, a silver chariot. It slowed and stopped. 'Going to the game, lads,' the driver enquired. Before he had finished asking we were in his vehicle and heading for Preston. As we sped along the motorway I took more notice of my surroundings and especially the driver. 'You're him aren't ya mate,' I pointed at the driver. It was, indeed, Ian Callaghan, ex-Liverpool and, of course, Swansea City. This was a message from God. Ian told us he was late because of the traffic coming out of Birmingham, he couldn't believe that so many Swansea fans had made the journey to Preston. At the time we were not to know that over 10 000 of us would be packed into Deepdale that afternoon, all shouting the Swans on to promotion. Fair play to Ian, he said he would pick us up and drop us off again at the services after the game. Maybe it would not surprise you that we were never to see him again, still, he had got us to the ground with two minutes to spare. We had made it.

During those heady days, we were up for almost anything for a laugh and Rowey, a good mate of mine, bet me on the way to the game that I could not get a shopping trolley into the ground. We had already managed to get twenty kippers into Luton, which were eagerly distributed amongst the travelling Swansea fans, and, amazingly, two deckchairs into Bristol City. The challenge was on. A local shop, not 20 yards from the visitors' end, had a number of shopping baskets outside, and on closer inspection I saw a trolley inside the store. It was borrowed for the afternoon. Up to this point I had not even given a minute's thought to how to get the damn thing into the ground, all that mattered was I had one, but what to do? I will never forget Dai 2's words to me, 'Chuck the bugger over.' He meant over the wall to the side of the turnstile. I hoisted it over the wall after two attempts, just before two members of the local constabulary came around the comer. Well, it was in there somewhere. Once inside the atmosphere was electric to say the least, there were thousands of Swans' fans in the ground, and they were in full voice. The trolley was resting on a metal gate and I grasped a hold of Rowey and showed him the trolley. He burst out laughing and reluctantly, a week later, coughed up the £10. Sorted. The game is well documented and we won 3-1.

Book the Linesman

Football has brought more than just a smile to a lot of our faces, the comments made by fans when in despair or in a moment's desperation have left me creased up, and the sights, some of the sights have left me speechless. I love the stories that fans have to tell about visits to places throughout the country. A good footballing buddy of mine recalled a visit to Scarborough one evening to watch Swansea play. It was not long after Scarborough had moved in to the Mcaan Stadium and the ground had made quite a lot of press. The Scarborough team were sponsored by Black Death vodka at the time and played in black. They took to the field in a black strip with the words 'Black Death' emblazoned on the front. Now this, to my mind, is superb, what a psychological edge this must have given them at times. Sadly, the Football League stopped them wearing the strip and having the logo on the front and they reverted back to a different garb, and back to relative obscurity. However, it was a certain character in the stand that made my mate stop, even if just for a moment. The stereotypical northerner has a flat cap and a whippet, especially in these parts. So to see a bloke of sixty plus and a whippet in the stand took a bit of getting used to. To cap it all, quite literally, he was wearing the customary flat cap, bless him.

I always stood in the same place on the Swansea North Bank for many years, and of course many others did as well. Now you get to notice certain individuals after a while, and some I got on nodding terms with. One in particular was an old boy who rarely spoke or muttered a word throughout the game. He always left with two minutes to go, which meant he missed quite a few goals in his time, and he also went to the North Bank 'serving hatch' for a cup of tea two minutes before half-time. Okay he smelled a bit, and had evidently been watching the Swans for a long time, but it bugged me to know for how long. One evening game I decided to have a chat with him, after all I had been standing next to him for nearly seven years. I asked him how long he had been watching the Swans. He told me since 1937 and for the next five minutes I couldn't shut him up, it was as if he had been released from a lifetime of not being able to talk. In comparison with his usual quiet way, this was a bit worrying. The only thing he ever shouted was, 'Come on, you bloody buggers,' when the going was getting tough. What I have to say was that he knew shitloads of stuff about the Swans, an untapped source of knowledge, and he covered many topics over the next few weeks when we met on the North Bank. Concerning Swansea he was, in my opinion, the fount of all knowledge. My mates nicknamed him 'The Guvnor'.

Our parting as Swansea soulmates was a bit sad, in fact, the way we passed by was very sad indeed in many ways. I recall the game, it was in the late eighties and the Swans were playing Northampton Town. I took my place at about a minute past three and the ground was silent, everyone was observing one of those minute silences you get now and then when a famous footballing tragedy or moment is observed. I couldn't think at the time what it was for, it went and the game cracked on. At half-time I mentioned that the old boy was missing, but that was it, no real thought about the reason why. I rarely look at the match-day programme until I get home and later that night, before going to bed, I had a glance through the usual stuff in the pages of *The Swan*. At the back was a picture of the chap we had affectionately called 'The Guvnor'.

His name was Les Middleton. He was born in Morriston in 1920 and served for 22 years in the RAF, like myself, a member of the Provost Branch. I never knew that. He became a signwriter after leaving the services, as I had myself, I never knew that. His stay with signwriting lasted a further 20 years, mine a mere three. There seemed to be a lot more to this chap than he let on, but in typical Swansea fashion, the programme didn't actually say right until the end of the piece that he had died that week in hospital after being attacked in his home by a burglar. He was 69. He lived alone and for the Swans, I didn't know that either. So a great chap and a fellow Swans' fan had his life cut short by some scumbag who didn't know him and hadn't taken the time to get to know him. Les was a lonely man who lived for his 90 minutes on the Swansea North Bank, it was clearly all he had to look forward to. The atmosphere and brief moments of glory were his family and, of course, his memories. Les shared those memories with me and as I said, he knew loads. His life was probably not much to write home about, but he didn't deserve to die in the way he did. We all stand next to somebody like Les and they've all got stories to tell.

So What's it all About Then?

It's quite funny to hear people who are not football fans slag off the world's biggest game, in fact, I find it very amusing. 'Twenty-two poofs chasing a bag of wind about,' is a favourite. Another is, 'You don't get that sort of trouble at rugby matches.' Choose any of these or even, 'They are a bunch of girls, kissing each other,' add the rugby comment, and you have the moronic, anti-football bloke off to a T. I have seen many ways of dealing with this breed of person. The reaction of a mate of mine, who was getting some grief off a big, rugby-type bloke in our local one night, seems funny now, but didn't at the time. This brain-dead egg-chaser was giving it the usual garbage when my mate asked him if he thought the same of him, as a person, like. Did he think my mate was a poof or a girlie? 'If you're a football fan, you're a poof,' came the reply. 'Oh really,' says my mate and punched him really hard, straight in the mouth. The egg-chaser reacted in the slow manner you would expect, taking about ten seconds to react to the blow, and then collapsed in a heap on the floor. 'Who's a poof?' my mate asks, his point made, albeit not in the way I would condone. Still, as I said, looking back it was a funny moment.

You can't converse with the anti-footy mug, you have to take the Mickey, and to do this you have to have a little bit about you. Another mate, Paul, was a married man by the time he was seventeen, and his wife was a bloody monster, no other way to describe her. Paul was a Swansea season ticket holder and very rarely missed a game, that is until he got married. God, did she change him. For two years Paul did not darken the Vetch Field gates, completely under the spell of this awful woman. She would not allow him to go. Now if he was a bit of a shagger or spending all his hard-earned cash on beer and footy you might sort of understand, but the reality was she just didn't want him to go. And he didn't. Not that it stopped her servicing the town on her nights out, when Paul stayed at home looking after her two kids from her first marriage. This was her third and she was twenty-six by the way, very clever at the manipulation stakes. Paul was a generally placid bloke, but his sort is often the worst when they do go bang. And boy, did Paul go bang.

His lovely wife actually felt so confident in her control over Paul she brought 'a friend' home after another night out She was busying herself in the nether regions of this bloke's undergrowth when Paul came downstairs. He exploded. The bloke left the house via the bedroom window, upstairs that is, as did she. Both had broken bones, and Paul himself called the police and ambulance. He was arrested and charged. The marriage had reached a crucial stage. She, with a broken arm, returned to her pre-marriage pose of being a lovely lady, and seriously tried to get Paul to see she had repented and seen the error of her ways. He was having none of it. They were divorced, and surprisingly, the crucial bit that did it was not her elastic legs but football. Paul laid down a few rules for the continuance of the marriage such as no shagging about, and added his wish to return to the Vetch with the lads twice a month. She laughed and did the usual patting on the head routine, and thankfully Paul saw straight through it. He kicked her into touch. Since that day in 1980 he has missed five Swans' home games. He lives alone in a two-bedroom flat in West Wales, and the last time I saw him he never looked better. Top bloke.

Something we all have in common with Paul, although most stories don't finish in the happy way his does, is why do our partners, male or female, find football so intrusive in their relationships? Why do they try to control and eventually stop this healthy way of running their partners' lives? My understanding is that football or, more importantly, the team we support can totally mess us about for many years, they can lose at home 5-0, play like total tossheads or even spend years in the worst league in the world, and still we go to watch them. Very strange behaviour. Partners must find this loyalty hard to get to grips with, especially if that loyalty is not shown in their relationship.

Getting too deep? Let's make it easier. Compare Paul's happening with his misguided wife to a bit of a test of loyalty, why did Paul react in this way? To me, for two years she had taken the piss and, more importantly, cut off his only avenue of pleasure, football. Not only that, she had increased her avenues of pleasure at his expense. He reacted in a fairly normal way, I think most blokes with a semblance of pride would have done the same, to a certain degree, at least kicking her into touch. His loyalty had been tested. Now if this is the case, then why does he travel to, say, Hartlepool on a cold and windy February night, watch a dismal performance and still go back for more a few days later. He has been let down, spent nearly 24 hours on a round trip to watch utter garbage, spent nearly sixty pounds and all he does is quietly complain, or at the most shout a few obscenities at the players and manager. Not only this, it happens quite often. I spoke to Paul. In his own words, this is his reasoning behind his passion for football.

Paul's Story

After the wife left me, I found myself returning to the lads and the pub and all the things I had really missed since I married and divorced Elaine. She ruined my life for two years. It was only after I got back in to watching the Swans that I realised just how much I love the team and football. Christ, she wouldn't even let me watch highlights on the tele. Bitch. As luck would have it, I got back into watching the Swans as they rose to the First Division. I loved watching Alan Curtis, Robbie James, Leighton James and Bob Latchford in the white shirt. When I celebrated watching my first Swansea goal for ages, it was definitely better than sex, well, sex as I knew it. This makes up for all the times we miss sitters or get thrashed and you're 400 miles from home. The feeling you get when the Swans score cannot be described. I know all football fans feel the same way about their teams, we are not in any way different. Swansea can mess me about as much as they like, I will always be there, no matter what the weather. They certainly will not get any divorce petition from me. There is no way I could contemplate giving up on them, how could I? The trips to Wembley, the days out with the boys, FA cup-ties at Liverpool and Newcastle. I even went to Middlesboro in 1995, when we knocked their so-called star-studded team out of the FA Cup. It was brilliant.

I hate seeing a Swans player not giving 100 per cent, that really annoys me. No fan will abide this behaviour, that is definitely letting the team down. I also hate the idiots that run football clubs today, do they really think they can bluff us, the fans, with their bullshit? I can see right through them and I won't tolerate being lied to by these idiots. The supporters are the strongest thing a club has, we should realise just how strong we are, and, more importantly, the owners should be left in no doubt. I've never been happier than when I am watching the lads and when I am with the lads. This is better than marriage, trust me, I know. I gave my wife an ultimatum, she laughed and now she is my ex-wife, it's as simple as that really. I love Swansea City more than anything, and I will do anything for the club and the team. I don't care who plays for us as long as they give 100 per cent, like Steve Jones did in the play-offs against Chester at the Vetch. We swamped them that night, over 10 000 patriotic voices. Those few Chester fans at that game must have been really jealous. They never have had nor will they have support like ours. And I know deep down it will all come right again and there will be more nights like that and like Wembley. No one can take those memories away and that's the reason why I won't ever let anyone take them away again. Swansea till I die.

Paul's story is repeated around the country day in, day out – sheer, unadulterated emotion for their team. You can't fault people like that, they are the lifeblood of the game. Oh, and while I remember, Paul was convicted of the assault on his wife and the poor chappie she brought home to play with. He got 200 hours community service. See, there is a God and sometimes there is justice.

What Happens Next?

Football has changed dramatically at the top since the eighties and the disasters at Bradford, Heysel and Hillsborough. Premiership games bear little resemblance to the First Division terrace days of the early eighties, when violence was around many a corner, no matter where you went. It had to change, and if you have had the pleasure of visiting, say, Villa Park, Old Trafford or St James's Park, you will have seen dramatic changes in stewarding, policing and the basic attitude of football fans. Even the catering is scrutinised! Welsh football has not enjoyed these incentives – all three of the League clubs struggle in the 2nd and 3rd Divisions, with the threat of Welsh League football hanging over them from the fools who determine the future of the game. In a three-week period during January 1995, 85 000 people watched four Swansea City games: at the Vetch Field against Middlesboro, the replay at Ayresome Park, the next round tie at Newcastle and an Autoglass Trophy semi-final at St Andrew's Birmingham. The League of Wales attendance for all their teams for that season didn't even come close to that figure. Which seems to tell the turkey-necks at the League of Wales to look elsewhere to improve their dire league.

No matter who you support, and the more successful your team the more noticeable it is, you will always see the fair-weather supporter or the glory-seeker at a game. The foolish ones keep on about their loyalty, almost as if to try and convince themselves that they are the real McCoy. They are easy to spot, I saw loads at St James's Park when the Swans played there in the fourth round of the FA Cup a few years back. On the way to the ground, I noticed that in the 1980s Southend beat Newcastle 2-0 in the League Cup. It was at St James's Park and in front of 4800 people, hardly the passionate Geordie following that night, where were they? They were waiting in the shadows for success and glory. They are no different from other clubs. Cardiff City are a similar entity, they have an average gate in 1998 of 3500, Swansea the same, but if they were to do something their support at Ninean would be massive. Look at the Swans in the early eighties in the old First Division. They averaged 17 000 that season, and got a 24 000 crowd at home to Southampton, Man United, Arsenal, Liverpool and all. And we beat the bloody lot of them.

Cardiff City continually bang on about being a sleeping giant, I hope for Welsh football that they do realise their potential, and the Swans, of course, stay one step ahead. At the time of writing, Cardiff City, the sleeping giant, are in a coma that not even Dr Big Bollocks could stir them from. I hope that both of us do something of note, and quickly, before those fools at the Welsh FA and UEFA get their own way and condemn us to the League of Wales, with Abergavenny and Aberystwyth. No disrespect folks, but that particular league is for the likes of these teams, and they do not deserve to grace the pitch with the likes of Swansea and Cardiff City. And don't think a few half-decent results against mixed up Swans and Cardiff teams, in a poorly-supported Welsh Trophy, in front of a thousand people is a benchmark – cos it ain't.

Hey, I'm uniting the Swans and Cardiff here, do we have a similar goal? Of course we do. One that only real supporters of both teams have. Leave the morons out of it, they know nothing. The muppet shows of the Premier League (I mean the crowd), where the glory-seeker squirms in his seat like a pervert at the passion all these clubs have generating from the seated terracing, are good to watch. Sky TV has brought a billion-pound business into the homes of the wealthy and comfortable, and attracted millions in sponsorship from the world's biggest companies This is the rat race that football has let itself get into. And who can blame them, where else did they have to go? A return to the violence of before? No way, even I would rather see some spoilt brat clapping conservatively at another Andy Cole goal at Old Trafford than a return to the scenes we all witnessed not too long ago. And that sums up my final point, the reason why I'm a Jack and I hate the scum! I love Swansea City just as passionately as Paul does, maybe more, know what I mean?

I am not jealous of the Premiership clubs or their fair-weather supporters. I respect those Man United fans who travel the length and breadth of Europe supporting their team, especially those who stuck with the club through the less-than-glamorous seventies, they are being rewarded today for their loyalty. Fair play. I want success for Swansea but what price do I have to pay? What fool's bullshit do I have to endure as a consequence of success? How much will it cost? Will I get a seat and which fair-weather supporter will I get to sit next to – and have to stop myself from shouting very loudly, 'Fuck off, you're killing me!' Will I sit in the McDonalds' stand or the lovely, shiny Windscreens' stand – at the expense of stands of old like the Spion Kop and North Bank. Who knows, success breeds the most hated individual this fair game can give: the bullshitter chairman and his vision for the future. It's a spiel we have all heard at a dozen clubs with a hundred years' of tradition ready to be traded for the lure of filthy lucre.

When I look at it this way, maybe we are the real McCoy down at the lower end of things, maybe we are enjoying it more than Man United and Spurs, especially Spurs. How their fans can moan I don't know. Take a good look around you, boys, things ain't that bad. My club has given me everything and I have given equal in return. It has showed me life and, quite literally, showed me death. It has given me emotions that nothing else has ever come close to, I have cried and laughed, fought and shouted, and still I remain and they remain for me. We are one, we are the club, the soul, the future, the past and the present. I despise those who laugh at my club because that is an attack on me, and I don't like to feel threatened. Saturdays are sacred, but then so is every day I can watch football. But then I get a jolt, is it reality? I see awful things and I see genuine hardship and the misery it brings, then I see Swansea and it all falls into place. New ground, old ground, it matters not. As long as I can still watch my team, that is all that matters, and to be honest I don't really care where that is, as long as it's not in the League of Wales. Well, you have to keep some semblance of reality, don't you? Oh and, of course, a real grip of loyalty, that they can never take away. The memories – just like Les, I still have memories. Swansea till I die.

Chapter 5

1927: and the things that make me love ... Kiardiffffff!

The Bluebird of Bridgend

*"The mentality that is within us all.
He's your mate, not mine."*

Cardiff City are the premier Welsh club. Those tossers, the Jacks from Swansea are just pretenders to the throne. We have the best support and the most passionate supporters in the land, and that includes England. We won the FA Cup in 1927, the Jacks have never done that. We have always had the upper hand on them, no matter what you compare us in, we are the best. I hate the Jacks more than anything, I really do. Having said that, I also have a healthy respect for them, when I was younger they always turned out a good-sized crew against us and always gave us a good run for our money, no one else has. You have to respect them for that.

I have grown up somewhat since my younger days, I now take my young son to Ninean, and I feed off his passion for the blue shirt of Cardiff City. Listen, even when you say it means more and sounds better than Rochdale or Norwich. You choose, it will always sound better. My lad longs for the weekend and our trips to see Cardiff play. I even take him away from home these days. He is a diamond, a real Cardiff fan, just like I was when I was a kid. I remember seeing Man United at Ninean in the seventies and the massive support we had that day – this has to come back, it has to.

When the Jacks were in the old First Division I loathed them, okay, I was jealous. We were shit and are not much better now, but at least they are as well, now. I suppose it means that one day both us and the

This is it: the "big one" – there's no rivalry like it.

Jacks will disappear from view, or at least the Football League, but we will go shouting, believe me, we will. I can't envisage this happening, however, we will be back. Cardiff City have supporters all over the world, we have a massive support in London and the majority of Welsh people support us before the Swansea scum. What I hate most is the Welshman who supports both of us, the Valleys idiots who latch on to the big game, you know the football fan-type person. The Man United fan who is Welsh is a real tosser, they are loathsome creatures, travelling to Manchester when they should be at Ninean watching the Bluebirds. Swansea have a big Man United support, that's why they are tossers as well.

I am also proud to be Welsh, and I love my country and its traditions. There is no better sight than a hundred Welsh flags behind a goal, away with the national team, and all with Cardiff City on them. You don't get many Jacks watching the Welsh team play and I hate them for that as well. How can they turn out massive crews to watch their club side play and play up as good as Cardiff, and not follow their country? It mystified me, then a mate told me why. I thought it was that they were afraid of us. My mate told me that they have an underlying nationalistic influence in Jackland. Good, I thought, so why don't they turn out away in Europe. What he meant was they are proud to be British, more so than Welsh. Now this is worrying. I have seen Union Jacks and Ulster flags in the Swansea end at derby games, but never really put two and two together. These boys are no better than Chelsea, or even England. And then he tells me that they support Glasgow Rangers and all that shit, now I really hate them, they are Welsh for God's sake. Now I know not all you Jacks are like this, but why are a good number of you like this? I can't even get my head around this. Since then I have seen Swansea Union Jacks at England games and at Rangers. They even travel to Holland to watch Den Haag, but they don't follow Wales in any numbers, crazy people those Jacks. Fair enough, they sent a massive crew for the Holland game at the Arms Park a few years back and the German game, not compared to us mind, but decent enough in size. Bollocks to them, I hate them you know.

I spoke to Keith, the book's author, when he first had the idea for a book about Welsh football fans and liked him, then he told me he was a Jack as well. At least he is a real fan and he follows Wales. He reck-

ons us Cardiff fans are paranoid about Swansea and are always comparing ourselves to them, he reckons that is our downfall, made me think that. Then I find myself doing it, can't help myself. I just want to believe we are better than they are. Those Jack Bastards rioted at Ninean in 1993, tore up all the seats in the away end and threw them into the junior enclosure, attacking all the kids. They are the reason why we were both banned from games for four years. I hated to have to watch that, it was horrible. I wanted to kill 'em all. My dad, who is now 67, also hates the Jacks, and since that night he really hates them. They were allowed to come back in 1997, they were all bussed into Ninean by the police, only about a thousand of them. They kicked off as soon as they came into the ground, giving it the big one to the Bob Bank. It's strange really, as I said, no one does it to us except them bastards. I hate them for it. We will do the same to them when we go there, in fact, I reckon it will be some turnout from our lot, no problem there.

I went to Belgium a few years back to see the Bluebirds in the Euro Cup Winners Cup at Standard Liege, we turned out about 3000 that night. It was brilliant in the bars before the game, getting all the Belgies to sing 'Gas a Jack' and 'You Jack Bastard' at the police, all in good fun, though. I don't like the violent side of it these days, it's just the sense of belonging I like, just being there and all that.

I'm 45 now and still react to the game like I did when I was 15, still as passionate and still as loud. I have had some bollockings off the stewards and police, and was ejected for being noisy at Scunthorpe a few years back, but I've never hurt anyone or been arrested, maybe I'm lucky. Football violence is interesting. It's a bit like chess really, I want it to be clean and clinical, no injuries, that's not football. Now I've written this I'm a bit ashamed, I should know better.

My mates in work know my feelings for City and they have the same. I don't know why it is, it just is. Seeing thousands of Bluebirds at a game, all singing and cheering, is like a drug, it's addictive. I was at Reading in the FA Cup and was really surprised that the press reacted like they did because we got behind our team. They haven't seen real passion that's the problem and it scares them to death. Imagine if City were in the Premiership, it would be ace. Every week, thousands travelling to the English strongholds and outsinging them. That's my dream – just for one season. And I would love to see City play at Wembley, the Jacks took only 20 000 to Wembley for their last two trips in the Autoglass and play-offs, we would fill it, easy. We are the real sleeping giant. Wrexham reckon they are Wales's best club, this is utter rubbish, they may as well be on Merseyside. They aren't real Welshmen, imagine having rivals like Chester City and Shrewsbury Town, some derby game eh? All 4000 of them, must be great!.

Our rivalry with Swansea was not evident in the sixties when I first went to see City play. We were in the Second Division, they were more often than not below us. We didn't often meet, and when we did we usually won. We won the Welsh Cup more times in a ten-year period than they ever have. I don't really think the Swansea thing started until the mid-seventies. We used to take over Swansea in those days, they had very few lads back then. It was all off the cuff, not like today, organised offs on mobile phones and all the designer gear that you read about. I don't think I would enjoy that. What I loved was the uncertainty, the beer and the crack with the boys. Just being with the boys, giving it a show of strength at Chelsea in 1975, was ace. We were in their North Stand, they ran at us and we stood and cheered them. What a day out that was, I got home at 11am on the Monday.

'Cardiff boys are on the piss again.' There I go again, I should know better. The feeling you get at derby games is not like the normal feeling you get on a match day, there is definite uncertainty. I woke up in November 1997, the day the Jacks returned to Ninean, like a kid on Christmas Day. My boy had never seen the Jacks before and he was buzzing, that's partly my fault. He enjoyed all the atmosphere and the game and he cried when they scored. They were the luckiest team to come to Ninean that year – "Jammy Jacks".

Yes, I know I could go on but I just wanted to say a few things. I'm not a thug, I just love the buzz of being at City. Some of you will hate me, but I bet you have enjoyed reading this small piece about Cardiff City, especially the City boys. I've got loads more to say, but this is not the forum, maybe I will try and do it again. Maybe, and more likely I won't. All I know is that I love Cardiff City and I really hate Swansea.

C'mon you Bluebirds.

Chapter 6

Dreaming of Barcelona
Mick Lehane

The big three dabble with the giants of Europe.

Until 1993, Welsh club interest in European competition was limited to the European Cup Winners Cup – without a national league, this was the only competition available. Throughout the 1960s and 70s, Cardiff City dominated the Welsh Cup. Their European adventures were well received and the club acquitted itself well in the competition, twice being knocked out at the quarter-final stages, by Real Zaragoza in 1964-65 and by Real Madrid in 1970-71. The home game against Real Madrid on March 10th 1971 was one of Cardiff City's all-time great games. In front of 47 500 ecstatic supporters, City managed to win 1-0, with Brian Clark scoring. Some 25 years later, Clark is still dining out on that goal. City were beaten 2-0 in the second leg, but to beat the mighty Real Madrid will remain the Club's greatest European achievement. Real went to the final that year and lost to Chelsea.

Although the scalp of Real Madrid remains the ultimate, the 1970-71 cup run was not the club's most successful. In 1967-68, Cardiff were knocked out at the semi-final stage by HSV Hamburg, then of West Germany. On their way to the semi, Cardiff had accounted for Shamrock Rovers of the Irish Republic, the Dutch side Nac Breda and Moscow Torpedo of the USSR. The quarter-final game against Moscow went to a play-off in West Germany which Cardiff won 1-0. In the semi-final against Hamburg, Cardiff drew 1-1 away and appeared to have completed the difficult task. On May 1st 1968 they lost 3-2 at home, and lost their only real chance of European glory. The mighty AC Milan accounted for Hamburg in the final that year.

The four League clubs dominated the Welsh Cup at this time: Cardiff City, Wrexham, Swansea City and Newport County.

In truth, Newport's cup success and highlights are limited to one cup adventure, 1980-81. Newport had an easy start, beating Crusaders of Northern Ireland 4-0 at home. A 0-0 draw in Ireland was enough. In the second round, Haugar FC were beaten 6-0 at home, which put Newport County into the quarter-finals of the competition. This was an amazing achievement for a club who was struggling in the Third Division of the Football League that season. Newport were drawn against the East German side, Carl Zeiss Jena. The first leg was to be played away. It was a shock to everyone that County managed a 2-2 draw, both goals scored by Tommy Tynan, a prolific scorer for the club. It was hard to come to terms with the fact that Newport were 90 minutes away from the semi-finals of the Cup Winners Cup, and with two away goals in the bag, it once again seemed as if the hard work had been done.

CRISPIN LANE STAND
Enter at TURNSTILE No. 11 ONLY Crispin Lane
(See over for details)

ROW B   SEAT No.   31

EUROPEAN CUP WINNERS CUP
WREXHAM v. ANDERLECHT
WEDNESDAY, 17th MARCH, 1976.   K.O. 7.30

PRICE £1.50.   *C. N. Wilson.*
                              Secretary,
This portion to be retained.   Wrexham A.F.C.

Of course, it was not to be. The Germans proved to be too strong on the night and County were out. For a struggling club like Newport, the cup run was a bonus, their chance to mix it with the big boys of Europe. Of course, success on this scale makes you hungry for more.

Newport County vowed to return to the competition as soon as possible. Sadly, less than 10 years later, the club was no longer in existence. This was to be Newport's finest hour on the European stage. Years of mismanagement and broken promises followed. John Aldridge was given away to Oxford United for a ridiculous fee and without the protection of a percentage in any follow-on sale of the player. When Newport finally went under, Aldridge was being sold to Liverpool for one million pounds. Five per cent of that amount and Newport County might still be with us today.

The main fear of the Welsh League clubs during the early 1980s was to avoid English clubs in the Welsh Cup. Shrewsbury and Hereford were a constant threat. Of course, if they won the Welsh Cup, they could not enter the European Competition, so if you could avoid them along the way, then you were guaranteed the big pay day of European football – even when you lost the final. All you had to do was dish out a beating to the giants of Welsh League football, like Brymbo Steelworks or Lex XI, and everything else was plain sailing.

In the early 1980s, Swansea City were a First Division club; they had become the first Welsh club to qualify for a UEFA Cup place, by virtue of their finishing sixth in the First Division of the English League. The club has opted to represent England in the UEFA Cup but because they were Welsh Cup holders, they opted to represent Wales in the Cup Winners Cup. When a situation such as this occurs, is it any wonder that the rest of Europe is up in arms about the whole situation? How can a club from a national league of one country (England) be able to represent another country (Wales) in European competitions?

Swansea, even in their high-flying days as a First Division club, have never fared very well in European competition. They have never reached the dizzy heights of Cardiff or Newport, but they have had some memorable games along the way. The club's biggest win in their history was recorded in Europe, when they managed to blitz the mighty Sligma Wanderers of Malta 12-0. For good measure, they won 5-0 away to record a 17-0 aggregate win. But Paris St Germain were waiting in the next round and they proved to be far too good for the Swans. In 1991-92, Swansea were pulled out of the hat with AS Monaco of France who could boast the talents of Roger Mendy of the Cameroon, who had delighted the crowds at the World Cup in Italy during the summer of 1990. Also in the French club side was one George Weah. He was one of the superstars of European football at the time. Needless to say, Swansea lost heavily to the French side.

The Swans' most exciting European adventure came in the 1989-90 season. Against the Greek side Panathinaikos, in the away leg Swansea stunned their more illustrious opponents, coming home with a credible 3-2 defeat. Goals from Paul Raynor and John Salako made sure the tie was far from over. The return game at the Vetch was somewhat overshadowed by the after-match events in Athens. There was serious crowd trouble and the Swansea supporters who travelled felt that much of the violence towards them had been caused by the Greek supporters. The return game was billed as some sort of revenge mission and the police were out in large numbers. For the 8000 plus who attended the game, just getting into the crowd was an ordeal in itself.

I can never understand the police authority's logic when they have to have extra officers at a big game. On this occasion, all of the extra officers were from the Bristol area. They had no idea where entrance gates were situated, and in many instances only wanted to confront supporters who disagreed with their directions. Once you gained entry, you were subjected to more searches by overzealous boys in blue. The match itself was an absolute cracker – and Swansea can rightly claim that they should have won. Robbie James and Andy Melville (with two goals) had the Swans 3-1 up with only 10 minutes left, and when the Greeks pulled one back everyone expected Swansea to finish them off in extra time. Then this particular Greek tragedy was complete. With only a few minutes to go, Panathinaikos equalised and the dream of glory was gone for another year.

Of course, one of the great romances of domestic cup football is that all of the big boys will take a fall and one of the lesser lights will take centre stage. This happened in the Welsh Cup Final of 1986-87 when Newport County were much fancied to beat Merthyr Tydfil, who at this time played in the dizzy heights of the Southern league (Midland Division). Merthyr's road to the final had seen them account for Cardiff Corries, Maesteg Park, Caernarfon, Barry Town, then Bangor City in the semi-final, which eventually had to be decided on penalties. The cup run had seen Merthyr pitted against teams of their own standard or lower; Newport County were a Football League club. It was widely expected that Newport would win comfortably in the final at Ninian Park.

The game finished in a 2-2 draw, with Bob Latchford, once of Everton and England, getting one of the goals. Many felt that Merthyr had blown their chance: they would be beaten in the replay four days later in Cardiff. In fact, Chris Baird scored from the penalty spot and the rest is history.

If the players and supporters of Merthyr had thought they were in dreamland, God alone knows how they must have felt when the draw for the first round of the Cup Winners Cup took place in Geneva. Merthyr were drawn to play the Italian Cup winners, Atlanta. Even though Atlanta had been relegated from Serie 'A' the previous season, so they were in effect a Division Two team, they were still an Italian team and they boasted players who had played for some of the big Italian clubs. And they had the tall, blond Swedish international, Glenn Stromberg.

The much-hyped Italians must have considered themselves very lucky to progress to the second round of the competition. They scraped through. They were uneasy throughout the game at Merthyr and were glad they would have the second leg at home. Merthyr were just at the start of their golden era and the team quickly progressed through the non-league to reach the Vauxhall Conference. But it is to the Cup Winners Cup games with Atlanta that most Merthyr supporters turn when seeking the memory to be cherished.

In the years after Merthyr's exploits, normal service was resumed in the domestic cup competition, with the Football League clubs once again dominating. 1988-89 saw Cardiff City return to the competition. A first leg visit to Derby City of the Irish Republic ended 0-0, but the return leg at Ninian Park was a more predictable affair, with City running out easy winners at 4-0, with a hat-trick for Jimmy Gilligan. The main memory of the evening was the Derby City supporters who had followed their team in vast numbers, although Derby is in Northern Ireland. Because of the sectarian violence in the city, the club was forced to play in the Republic's League. For a club like Derby City, every game is a bonus, and the good-natured behaviour of their supporters was a joy to see. It is the only time I have seen supporters whose team has just lost 4-0 celebrate in such a fashion. I suppose for

Derry City just being in European competition was a victory over those groups in their home country who had forced them into exile. Cardiff's reward for their victory over Derry was a tie with Aarhus GF of Denmark.

Aarhus were certainly no giants of the European game, but they dispatched Cardiff with ease. The result came as no surprise to supporters, but even with Cardiff struggling in the Third Division at the time, it is hard to admit. For opposition teams to draw a Welsh club at this time meant easy passage to the next round. For the record, Cardiff lost 2-1 at home and were hammered 4-0 away. The crowd for the home game was just over 6000, which shows the people of Cardiff had lost interest in their club's European adventures.

The next European adventure was again a short-lived experience. In 1992-93, Cardiff once more carried the European flag for Wales. The draw saw the Australian Cup holders, Baumit Admira Wacker, as the opponents. The first leg was at home, where Cardiff managed a 1-1 draw, with a goal from Chris Pike. The game was such an abysmal showing that all of the talk amongst the supporters had been about the Government's interest rate rise of four per cent. It was a black Wednesday in more ways than one.

The return in Austria saw City lose 2-0 and another European adventure was over. Before September was out, once again Cardiff had been paired with less than glamorous opposition and again failed to make any progress (or, one suspects, any financial gain) as once again the crowd for the game only matched any average League game.

The warning signs were now clear to Cardiff and the other League clubs. There had long been complaints that Wales did not have a national league and this situation was corrected in 1992. The new League of Wales was a curiosity to many, who felt that it would not last a season. The Football Association of Wales said that Wales had to have its own league or it might risk losing its right to a national team. Much of what was said by the Welsh FA was treated with a certain degree of scepticism by the clubs. There were threats that they would all have to join the league because UEFA had decreed it. There was so much uncertainty that when the league eventually got under way, there was more interest in events off the field.

The Football League clubs had assurances from the Football Association of Wales that they would not be forced to join the national league; the same cannot be said for the non-league clubs. The whole sorry business eventually ended in the High Court, where the Welsh FA lost its court battle with the rebel clubs who had successfully claimed that to force them to play in the new league was, in effect, restraint of trade.

This long-running court case overshadowed the League of Wales and its eventual first winners – Cwmbran Town. Winning meant that Cwmbran would represent Wales in the European Cup. They were, therefore, Wales's first, and until this season (1997-98) only, club to play in Europe's premier club competition. Because of the expansion of Europe, Cwmbran had to take part in the preliminary round of the competition. No big names were available at this stage so, for the privilege of the first European cup-tie on Welsh soil, Cwmbran had to be content with Cork City – champions of the Irish Republic. Cwmbran were very much the underdogs but they more than matched their Irish visitors and were good value for their 3-2 win. It was only fitness level than let them down in the end, and allowing Cork to go home only one goal behind was a flattering scoreline.

In the return game in Ireland, Cwmbran were again unlucky and the Irish eventually won the match on their own ground. Cork City went on to play Galatasay of Turkey and were unlucky not to progress further in the competition. The Turkish side then beat Manchester United. This sequence of events left Cwmbran wondering what might have been, for them it was very much a case of so near and yet so far.

In the same season, Cardiff again played in the Cup Winners Cup and this time the draw was kinder to them in terms of quality of the opposition. Their opponents were Standard Liege of Belgium and the first leg was to be played away. This is always a popular choice for managers – hopefully, you can keep a clean sheet and perhaps steal an away goal. On this occasion, Standard Liege opened the scoring but Cardiff shocked them with two goals from Tony Bird. To many Cardiff City fans, the glory days of European football were on the way back. 2-1 up away from home against a team who were fancied in the competition. Just as the fans were dreaming of who they were going to play next, the roof fell in on their dreams. The Belgians were stunned to be losing on their own ground and by full time they had redressed the balance to win comfortably by 5-2.

The return leg with Cardiff was a predictable affair and the European dream again ended at the first hurdle. The fans were unaware at the time that this was to be the club's last European adventure, unless, of course, they resign from the Football League and play in the National League of Wales. It was a sad end to Cardiff's European involvement – from the 60s where there was real hope of at least a quarter-final slot to the 90s where European football had become a one-game nightmare. The only hope among the supporters was that you would face one of the European big boys and at least the club would benefit financially.

Following Cwmbran's European adventure, the Football Association of Wales decided that only clubs who played in the League of Wales or its feeder leagues could now represent Wales in European competitions. This meant the end of the road for the League clubs of Cardiff City, Swansea City and Wrexham. The non-league clubs like Merthyr Tydfil and Newport were also excluded because they opted to play in the English pyramid system, and this meant exclusion from all Welsh competitions. In Newport's case, you had the situation where they were excluded from the country altogether. They were not allowed to play in Wales at all and were forced to play in Gloucestershire. Thankfully, this situation has now been resolved and the club has returned to Newport.

The Welsh League's clubs now had two places in Europe to play for plus the pre-season inter-TOTO Cup. Despite all the efforts to discredit the league, mainly by the media, it has raised the hopes of every club that takes part.

One of the clubs which has benefited most from its association with the League of Wales is Barry Town, one of the original clubs who refused to take part. It has now become one of its leading lights. Barry has, in the past few seasons, become by far the best club in the League of Wales. They are its only full-time professional club, and because of this, have become almost untouchable in domestic competitions. They completed the treble in 1996-97, a season which also saw them enjoy European glory and the media attention which goes with it.

Because of the increased greed of UEFA, Barry Town was prevented from taking their place in the European Cup as Welsh champions. They were instead awarded places in an expanded UEFA Cup competition, but they were handsomely rewarded for foregoing the rewards of the European Cup. So, I suppose they were winners whichever way you look at it – paid not to take part in the European Cup but allowed to play in the UEFA Cup. Either way, they could not lose.

Dinaburg of Latvia were beaten in the first qualifying round, following a 0-0 draw at home. Barry secured a 2-1 win away. Then it was Budapest Vasutas of Hungary in the second qualifying round. Having lost 3-1 away, many thought that it was all over for Barry in the home game. Barry gave an outstanding performance to win 3-1 and forced the game into extra time. The game was undecided at the end of extra time so it was down to a penalty shoot-out. Barry's stand-in goal-keeper, Pat Mountain, proved to be the match winner, and now Barry could look forward to a first round game with Aberdeen. Barry lost the first game 3-1, and again many saw the return tie as a formality for the Scottish side. On the night, Barry were by far the better team and the eventual score of 3-3 more than flattered Aberdeen.

The League of Wales' standing was enhanced by Barry's performance. Many of those who had mocked the new league were now quiet. By insisting that Wales form its own national league, the Football Association of Wales had increased the aspirations of every small club in the country. Teams like Ton Pentre, Inter-Cardiff (now inter-CabelTel) and Ebbw Vale have all enjoyed their European trips. The League's critics will argue that with the exception of Barry, all of the others have fallen badly, but this is very much splitting hairs. For any club or player, the ambition must be to play at the highest possible level. To be able to play in European competition is the ultimate prize, whatever the outcome. The experience gained can never be taken away.

It is true that for all Welsh clubs, European football will continue to be an early season experience followed by a quick exit. But surely it is better to have the experience than have nothing at all? What is wrong with hoping for the big draw to secure your season financially? Dreaming of Barcelona is what football is all about!

Chapter 7

A Short Message from Carmarthen

Paul Ashley-Jones

"Go west, young man."

They say that a football club's most fanatical supporters often live away from the club itself. Born in Carmarthen, I've never lived in Swansea, and until recently had lived outside Wales for the last 10 years. But it hasn't stopped me supporting 'my' club. Although time and expense often means matches are followed by Ceefax or radio, there are always occasions, such as derby games or cup-ties, when you just have to be there. This caused few problems when I was living in Leicester and when I spent four years in London. Things were a bit more difficult between 1992 and 1995, when we lived in Germany. While I would plan holidays home to coincide with as many games as possible, there were two particular occasions when I had to make specific trips back just for the game itself. The later trip was Wembley in 1994, probably the greatest day 1've ever had as a Swansea fan. However, enough has been written about that match and my story concerns the first trip back, to Nuneaton Borough in November 1993.

Swansea had been very lucky to get a last minute equaliser in the first round of the FA Cup at the Vetch. The omens for the replay were not good and I actually felt that we'd lose. I don't know why I wanted to go, but for whatever reason, I just had to be there. I flew to Heathrow on the day of the game and arranged to meet two friends from Leicester at Nuneaton Station. We found our way to the ground and went to get tickets. You can imagine my delight to be told it was an all-ticket game and that there was no way in. They were kind enough to sell me a programme though, 'to give us something to read on the way home'. What nice people we thought! I poured my heart out to no

A certain Frenchman in a Swans shirt? If only . . .

Welcome to Swansea, 1998: the North Bank beckons!
(One day, my son may take his rightful place here - KH.)

avail, until a Swansea policeman told us to sit tight while he went to see what could be done. Now I have a lot of respect for our local police force but, with only an hour to kick-off, I wasn't about to hang around so I set off on a ticket search of my own. I managed to convince some local stewards that I had an appointment with the commercial manager, whose name I'd got from the programme. Once inside I managed to convince him that he had three tickets put aside for me that I'd booked earlier. I returned triumphant to my friends, waved the tickets at the programme-seller and disappeared into the local pub.

A few minutes before kick-off and I'm grabbed by the Swansea policeman on the way into the game. He was not pleased. He had found Robin Sharpe, Swansea's Chief Executive, who had managed to get three tickets for us and had spent 30 minutes in the freezing cold waiting to give them to me. I was very apologetic and made a feeble excuse about being moved on by the local force. I did write and thank Robin Sharpe afterwards but, although I shouldn't say it, the thought of a senior official freezing to death outside while we were enjoying a pint in front of a log fire, still brings a smile to my face.

Of course, we lost, despite leading with an early Torpey goal. The evening had one final twist, however. Nuneaton equalised to take the game into extra time. I realised with horror that if I stayed I would miss the last train back to London, and my flight back to Germany the next morning. I had little choice but to say my goodbyes and leave. The local radio was covering the game and I heard Nuneaton's second goal in the taxi on the way to the station. Cornforth missed a penalty as I was getting out of the cab. As the train made its way to London, the irony of the situation hit me. I had travelled all that way to see the game and wouldn't know the final result until the morning papers. If I'd stayed in Germany I would at least have got the result on Sky. I didn't know whether to laugh or cry, which sums up my 15 years of following the Swans rather well, actually.

Ever since I became a father, one of the things I have always looked forward to was the thought of taking my children to the footy. I've done all the usual proud parental things. Within days of being born my two boys were signed up with the Junior Supporters' Club. Both have been kitted out in Babygros with the club badge on. True, they never fitted that well and my second son did develop a rash after wearing one, but there you go. But nothing would compare to the day my eldest son would be old enough for me to take him to actually watch my team, the team I have followed over the last 16 years, my beloved Swansea City.

As that day grew nearer I eased him in gently, taking him to the occasional Carmarthen Town game in the League of Wales. He'd enjoy watching for a while, and could then kick a ball around with the other kids when he got bored. I began to feel that he was ready for the Swans. And that's where the first seeds of doubt began to cross my mind. As I looked back over the last 16 years, I began to analyse just what following the Swans has given me. I was 15 when I was deemed old enough to travel the 30 miles from Carmarthen to home games by train, with friends. Then I could attend regularly. Prior to this I was only able to go with my father, and he worked on Saturdays. In my first full season, 1982-83, we were relegated from Division One. No games against the Liverpools and Man Uniteds next year then, but I knew we'd bounce back. We were relegated again the following year.

All in all, the last 16 years have seen me witness four relegations and just the one promotion, in 1988 when we sneaked into the Division Four play-offs and beat Torquay in the final. (This was the first season of the play-offs and before the finals were played at Wembley. I couldn't get a ticket for the second leg and had to listen to the promotion on the radio.)

During this time I've watched some truly appalling football, seen my club go bankrupt, suffered 8-0 defeats at Liverpool and Monaco, and been humiliated at the hands of Bognor Regis and Nuneaton in the FA Cup. I can't even bring myself to estimate how much it has all cost me, financially or emotionally. On top of this I've had to endure the ridicule, or worse, sympathy of family and friends as we have lurched from one crisis to another. I can still see Kevin Cullis's face (remember him – former Cradley Town youth team coach and Swans manager for a bizarre week last season) when I close my eyes at night. On top of this I am surrounded by the Welsh media who waste no opportunity to put down 'soccer' whilst giving saturation coverage to rugby at all levels.

Was I really prepared to push my own children down such a route, to put them through the pain and humiliation their father has suffered, and will no doubt continue to suffer. What about school, with all their friends supporting one Premiership club or another? Children can be so cruel and should I leave my sons open to ridicule at such a young age? Hell, yes! It will be character building (probably). And there have been good times. Victory at Wembley in the Autoglass Trophy in 1994. Away wins, including this season, at Cardiff. Knocking Bryan Robson's Middlesborough out of the FA Cup at Ayrsome Park. Anyway, after an appalling start we're going well at the moment. Settled in a play-off position, Jan Molby had Swansea playing neat, attractive football. It was with this in mind that on February 15 1997 I took my three-year-old son Jake to Vetch Field for the match against Scarborough.

We sat in the family stand, waited for kick-off and surveyed the scene. The crowd was fairly poor, due mainly to Wales's rugby game in France being on the telly. Scarborough brought 38 fans with them – Jakey counted them. Who said football can't be educational? We kicked off. 'Will there be a penalty, dad?' (Jakey has a thing about penalties.) 'We'll see,' I replied. Four minutes later and we scored from a penalty. We cheered and hugged each other. He was getting cold and I gave him my Swans scarf, the one my father had bought for me at my first game. Any lingering doubts I had about bringing him had long since vanished. The rest of the game was awful. Rumours had spread that Molby was leaving following an argument with the chairman over the failure to sign a striker from Bristol City the day before. The team played with no heart and lost to a late goal. I had seen it all before but it hurt more today. Jakey had given up on the game by half-time and was more engrossed in a Mister Men colouring book.

We made our way out after the game, listening to fans calling for the chairman's head. 'Why didn't we win dad?' 'We don't always,' I replied, with an irony that was thankfully lost on him. 'We did score a penalty though,' he responded enthusiastically. I smiled. It was probably better this way. To see City win and believe it to be the norm would probably be worse for him in the long run. At least now he would know what to expect and maybe, sensibly, reject it outright. Perhaps he would be better off supporting Newcastle or whoever, as long as it's not rugby I wouldn't mind. But, of course, it doesn't work like that, does it? As we reached the car, still clutching his programme, he turned to me. 'I had a really nice time, dad.' The guilt overwhelmed me. 'Yes, I know you did, son. Sorry.'

Chapter 8

That's Why I support Hereford United

Chris Jones

A nostalgic journey which starts in South Africa and ends in tears at Edgar Street, Hereford.

Saturday, 3rd May at 4.50pm. The final whistle blows at Edgar Street on the final day of the season, and Hereford United have drawn 1 -1 with Brighton and Hove Albion. The teams had been level on points (after the FA invoked a previous suspended sentence and deducted two points from Brighton following a pitch invasion), but Brighton had scored more goals, so only a win for Hereford would be good enough. This was the way our 25-year stay in the Football League came to an end. A couple of days later I was given the brief to write what I liked about life as a Hereford supporter, which in a way is an invitation to recall the better times of my experiences following the Bulls. It will undoubtedly also set me thinking about what might have been. I make no apologies if this comes across heavy on sentimentality, but I was told to make it 'warts and all'.

I was born in South Africa in 1962, and lived there until the age of 20. Like any other football-mad seven-year-old, I followed an English team as well as a South African one. The English teams chosen were usually the League Champions or FA Cup Final participants, and I was no exception to this rule. Unlike several of my friends, who attached themselves to Chelsea after the 1970 Cup Final, I was the awkward one who chose Leeds United! It was a couple of years later that I became aware that my parents had friends who lived in a place called Hereford, which I hadn't heard of. My dad told me that Hereford had a football team that wasn't in the League, but had beaten Newcastle United of the First Division. Considering that this was the same season in which Leeds beat Arsenal to win the Cup, it seemed that I was destined to form some sort of allegiance to Hereford. The next four years were spent mainly concentrating on the trials and tribulations of Leeds, with the high of the 1974 League Championship being counteracted by the 1973 FA Cup Final defeat by Sunderland and the 1975 European Cup stitch-up by Bayern Munich. My memory of the day after the latter is of kicking a panel out of our kitchen door after hearing the circumstances behind the match, and, rightly, being told off!

The following year was dominated by my first holiday in Europe, running from the end of July until the middle of September – coinciding nicely with the start of the football season. By an outrageous stroke of fortune, we were staying in Hereford at the time of the match at home to Hull City, which was the club's first in the old Second Division. I persuaded my dad to take me, and then listened as he repeated what he had told me many times before – that football in England was of a much higher standard than I was used to watching in Johannesburg. This match was a real eye-opener for me in several ways. Firstly, I had never stood at a match before. Secondly, singing and chanting is not part of spectator-culture in South Africa, and I vividly remember the United fans giving an injured Hull player 'the count' when he was down for more than ten seconds! My only other recollection of the match itself is of Dixie McNeill hitting the bar and then scoring the only goal of the match. Dad remembered a farmer seeing the lush state of the pitch during the long dry summer and threatening to bring his cows down to graze on it! He also apologised to me for unintentionally misleading me about the quality of the football, as this was definitely the exception to what he had previously told me!

Two more years were spent following the declining fortunes of Hereford from 6000 miles away as the club went from the Second to the Fourth Division in successive seasons. Our family then paid another visit to these shores. Once again a visit to Hereford was a central point of the holiday, and one Tuesday night found our hosts and ourselves watching a play at the Nell Gwynne Theatre, which is right on the opposite side of Edgar Street from the ground. I can't remember what the play was but I managed to persuade everyone that I wasn't enjoying it that much, and that they should meet me after United's friendly with Wolves, which Wolves won 2-9. The other match I saw on that holiday was the Charity Shield in which Liverpool beat Arsenal 3-1, including a goal from Kenny Dalglish which for several more years was the best I had ever seen.

One more visit to England came at Christmas 1981, and although my friend and I saw several matches, the Arctic conditions that winter prevented a few more, including Hereford v Aldershot on Boxing Day. Back in South Africa, I continued to take a keen interest in local football and went to matches most weekends. At that time it was quite rare for whites to watch football because of the real threat of racial violence, but I still went, probably against my better judgement! In the early 1980s the new Ellis Park rugby stadium was built. It staged occasional football matches when other grounds weren't big enough to accommodate the expected crowds. The first of these saw my team (Jomo Cosmos) play against Orlando Pirates. We won the match 1-0 with an overhead kick by Frank McGrellis in the second minute, which naturally led us to christen the stadium McGrellis Park! It was a few months later that I discovered that McGrellis used to play for Hereford, and we used to spend the aftermath of matches discussing Hereford's chances of surviving re-election when the inevitable bottom four finish occurred!

My days in South Africa were numbered as my dad had always planned to return to live in England (he was from Portsmouth) when he retired in 1983. The move took place in June 1983 and my first priority was to find some work, which unfortunately took until April 1984. At the time I still considered myself a Leeds United supporter first and foremost, but with the lack of a job cramping my ability to travel to Elland Road or anywhere else on a regular basis, I started to watch Hereford. The transport costs were non-existent and admission was cheaper, although there wasn't the huge price difference between the higher and lower divisions that exists now. My first Hereford match as a resident of the city was a Milk Cup match at home to Portsmouth, who included the soon-to-be-famous Mark Hateley. United won the match 3-2 (but lost 3-1 in the second leg), but my abiding memory of the match was directing a lone chorus of 'You're gonna get your f***ing heads kicked in' at the Portsmouth fans when they scored. I thought that was what supporters did in those circumstances!

At that time I was also starting to visit different grounds towards the eventual '92 Club' so I didn't watch United away until February 1984. Like most people I suppose, my first away match was a local derby. In Hereford's terms, a local derby is anything under about 60 miles away, so Bristol City at Ashton Gate qualified as such. Bristol City won 1 – 0 en route to promotion at the end of the season. Three days later I was on the coach to the Welsh Cup quarter-final against Cardiff City at Ninian Park, where we outplayed them to win 3-1 – the first of many happy memories from that ground.

Very early in my Hereford-watching career I became aware of the England/Wales rivalry with the way the crowd was pumped up for the League match at home to Wrexham. It was the first of three matches between the teams within the space of eleven days and resulted in a 3-0 win, which gave us hope of success in the next two, which were the Welsh Cup semi-final. After drawing 0-0 at home in the first leg, we lost to a goal in the last minute of extra time at the Racecourse Ground. At this match I saw the first hints of the trouble which was never far from the surface when the teams met, even if it was only the hilarious sight of nine Hereford fans chasing the home fans across their Kop!

As is the case with all new seasons, 1984-85 brought its usual optimism, but this time it had some basis. The first month of the season was glorious, with United not conceding a League goal until October! The toughest test during this period came at Swindon, especially when the home team was awarded a penalty. Kevin Rose saved it to set us up nicely for the second half, during which we destroyed them to win 3-0. Farnborough Town were easily beaten in the first round of the FA Cup, and the draw sent us to Plymouth in the second round. Interest was so great that the club organised a special train, which was a great success. This was in the days when the third round draw was made after the match (which ended 0-0), and pandemonium would not be too strong a word to describe the scene on the train when we heard, 'Hereford United or Plymouth Argyle will play..Arsenal.' The replay was a superb night in which we saw off the Pilgrims to win 2-0 and set up the dream.

The club obviously introduced a voucher scheme for tickets for the Arsenal match, and this inflated the attendances for the next two home matches – Halifax Town and Aldershot. It was helped by the fact that United were doing well in the League at the time and the attendance for the Aldershot match was 8536, the second highest in the Fourth Division that season. Boxing Day saw us heading east to Colchester where, after a 2-2 draw, our coach was bricked on the way out of the town. Normally this would have been bad enough in itself being the middle of winter, but it became distinctly uncomfortable when we reached Cheltenham and it started snowing! Ten days later came the day we had been waiting for, and it was icy everywhere! It often is when small clubs play big clubs in the FA Cup. Going into Hereford before the match was incredible as most of the shops were either closed or boarded up! The club had erected a temporary stand to cope with the demand for tickets from United fans, and the home sections of the ground were packed solid. Unfortunately the away end wasn't quite as full as Arsenal returned 1600 of their 4600 tickets, which rightly led to them being ridiculed. The total attendance was 15 777.

The match was typical of the David and Goliath cup matches, with plenty of noise and passion, but we were speechless when Tony Woodcock scored a cracker from 25 yards. However, we were level before half-time after Chris Price scored following a passing move down our right-hand side. The second half was all Hereford, and only John Lukic and the effects of the rock-hard pitch (ironically) saved Arsenal from a hammering. Following the success of the special train to Plymouth in the previous round, the club laid on another one for the replay at Highbury, and then laid on two more to cope with demand! The original date for the replay passed uneventfully as the match was postponed due to snow, although we suspected that an injury to Kenny Sansom might have had a bearing on the decision as most of our penetration had come down that side. Eventually the match was played, and the whole day and night was one long disaster for Hereford supporters. Due to the abysmal quality of the trains British Rail provide for specials, they started to break down by the time we reached Swindon, and a series of crawls and lengthy delays ensued, which continued all the way to London. All three trains arrived late and some people didn't get to the ground until half-time, by which time we were 4-0 down! Things improved in the second half, which we lost only 3-2, but the 7-2 defeat was still the heaviest in our history.

The next match we played was again away, at Cardiff in the Welsh

Cup. Although we were two divisions below them, we outplayed them to win 4-0, which unfortunately was as good as it got for the rest of that season. Our League form remained quite good, and we were one of five teams with a realistic chance of being promoted. At the beginning of March we played Bury at Edgar Street – they were one of the other promotion contenders. It was a thrilling match with attacking football from both teams for the entire 90 minutes. With time running out we were hanging on for dear life to a 4-3 lead when Paul Maddy broke out of defence and ran the length of the pitch to score and clinch a memorable win. Our form tailed off, but with a couple of weeks left we were still in with a shout. We had to win away at Blackpool. The high stakes and the prospect of a weekender saw 1000 Hereford fans making their way north to boost the crowd to 8855. This was only 49 more than our crowd at home to Aldershot, but it still gave us involvement in the two largest crowds in the division for that season. The match was lost 2-0 and we finished fifth in the League, which we were never to improve on. The final match was away at Aldershot, and British Rail made up for the Arsenal fiasco by laying on a free train.

The 1985-86 season began with a testimonial for our Football Administrator, Jim Finney, who later was to amuse us all by forgetting to enter the FA Cup when he moved to Worcester City. The testimonial match was at home to the FA Cup holders, Manchester United. They brought down a useful-looking team, which beat us with a goal by Jesper Olsen after Chris Turner had kept us out with several superb saves. The first League match was away at Mansfield, who easily beat us 4-0. The first two home matches were dream wins against reasonably local rivals. In the first round of the Milk Cup we thrashed Bristol City 5-1, and Swindon Town were beaten 4-1 in the League. We lost the second leg against Bristol 2-0, but set up a repeat against Arsenal, with the first leg at Edgar Street ending 0-0.

After the previous season's hammering we were understandably apprehensive about the second leg, but surpassed our wildest expectations by taking the lead through Ian Wells in the 23rd minute. Arsenal equalised a minute later but there was no more scoring before 90 minutes, so extra time was necessary. I don't understand why extra time applies in the second leg as this gives the home team an obvious advantage, and I still think to this day that we should have gone through on the away goals' rule. As it happened, we came within six minutes of doing so anyway, then Charlie Nicholas rammed the chants he always used to be subjected to back down our throats. This was yet another of those seasons when we never really threatened to get promoted, so interest was restricted to the various Cup competitions.

The first round of the FA Cup was away, against old rivals from the Southern League, Yeovil Town. This was my first experience of following United to an away match at a non-league ground, and I was staggered by our support. The town of Yeovil was as well, as the trouble in the town that day was regarded by the locals as being worse than when they played Millwall! The match was played in a downpour, which encouraged most of the United fans to crowd into the covered section along the side of the pitch. This area became overcrowded, and when we scored just before half-time the pressure on the wall in front of us caused it to collapse, luckily without serious consequences. With five minutes to go and the score at 2-2, my first thought was what to do if the match went to extra time, as I had tickets to see Madness in Gloucester that night. Fortunately, Mike Carter scored twice in those five minutes to complete his hat-trick and give us a 4-2 win. The second round threw up a visit to Reading, where there had been serious trouble at the first round matches two seasons previously. The trouble wasn't repeated to any real extent but the result was, even to the scorers, Trevor Senior and Dean Horrix.

The Welsh Cup campaign had started with a 2-0 win against Bangor City, with both goals scored by Ollie Kearns, who later missed a penalty. Next up were BSC Shotton, who were thumped 10-1. By now the Freight-Rover Trophy had started, and in a match held up by a power-failure, United beat Bristol Rovers 2-0, which virtually ensured our qualification for the knockout stages. This was ensured by a 1-1 draw at Swindon. The quarter-final of the Welsh Cup paired us with Merthyr Tydfil, but we had a comfortable 3-1 win at Penydarren Park to set us up for something that we would become used to in the competition, a draw against Kidderminster Harriers. Further progress had also been made in the Freight-Rover Trophy after wins at Orient and at home to Swansea (on penalties), so we were in the Area Final as well as the Welsh Cup semi-final.

The first of these matches was away at Kidderminster, who outplayed us to win 4-1. In the second leg we were 3-0 up in the last minute and going through on away goals, but Kevin Rose came for a through-ball and changed his mind. He could only watch as the ball went over his head and landed in the empty net. The last two matches we played in the season were for the Area Final of the Freight-Rover Trophy. The first leg at Edgar Street ended in a 2-0 win and all was well with the world, although the night was spoilt by serious trouble before, during and after the match. Four days later, at Ashton Gate, the score was 0-0 with 30 minutes to go, but Bristol City scored twice in a minute to take the match into extra time. Shortly after hitting the bar, we conceded the winning goal in the 117th minute, and the club's elusive first Wembley appearance had gone. Considering the state of the game with 30 minutes left and what had happened against Kidderminster, it really was a shattering blow.

In the later stages of the 1985-86 season I bought my first car, an N-reg Citroen Dyane which looked and sounded like an upturned pram, but was capable of maintaining a decent speed given the right conditions. On 17th October 1986 1 passed my driving test, and five days later was driving three others up to Spotland (!) on a wet and windy Wednesday night. Conditions were horrendous, especially given my lack of experience of driving – there were stages when the lights were barely visible and the windscreen wipers only just coped! To make our night complete, we lost 2-0. November was a pivotal month in many ways. Our interest in the FA Cup ended in a 4-0 replay defeat at Craven Cottage. This followed a 3-3 draw in the first match, when the score was 2-2 after 20 minutes. The replay was memorable for two reasons – Ollie Kearns getting sent off for elbowing a Fulham player, after seemingly showing his elbow to the referee! The more pleasant reason was meeting a girl called Sarah on the terraces. She was to become a constant companion for the next few months. Sarah was my second consecutive girlfriend who I had met through football, earlier Mandy and I had enjoyed pleasant times watching United before illness curtailed her hobby – and ultimately her life. The first match Sarah and I went to was a 1-0 home defeat by Wrexham in the Welsh Cup, but the second was a superb 4-0 victory over our closest rivals (Newport County) in the Freight-Rover Trophy. The match was notable for being the debut appearance by Phil Stant, who scored a hat-trick. Boxing Day was one of those glorious days when close rivals get sent packing – in this case the mighty Wolverhampton Wanderers were beaten 2-0. It was about this time that I began to dislike standing where Sarah stood as the supports for the seats above us took out quite a lot of the view. This area is now the overflow for away fans, so for anyone who has had the misfortune of having to stand there, you have my apologies, especially as it is only used when there are a lot of away fans!

A month later I was at home on a Friday afternoon and night, feeling very sorry for myself and trying to convince myself that I would be well enough to go to Burnley the following day. I woke up on Saturday morning far from 100%, but decided that I would be miserable as well as ill if I didn't go to the match. Along with Sarah and my friends Nigel and Elaine (United fans from Cardiff), just before kick-off I took my place at a sparsely populated Turf Moor. Not only were there only about 60 Hereford fans, but the total attendance was only 1955! This was the season they got low crowds all season until the last match, when they had over 15 000 for the match they had to win against Orient to stay in the League. Going back to Turf Moor, the match was a dream as United scored their biggest League win (6-0). The highlight of the match was the best goal I have ever seen. Jimmy Harvey knocked a cross-field pass to Stewart Phillips on the right wing. Phillips put over a cross which Ollie Kearns met on the volley to send a screaming shot into the top corner of the net! Having seen Kearns miss quite a few easier chances in preceding years, it was quite a surprise to see the net bulging as it did. As it happened, I wasn't well enough to drive home, but luckily Elaine had a licence and was able to help by driving home in the fog.

Two nights later we were at Molineux for the first round of the Freight-Rover Trophy, and a goal by Kearns gave us our second victory over Wolves in a month. A further two days later we beat Crewe Alexandra 2-0 in the League – and then lost eight successive matches! The highlight of the rest of the season was a last-minute equaliser at Wrexham to deny them a place in the play-offs. Our last match was away at Cambridge United, which we lost 2-1 after arriving late due to the traffic on the winding roads around Cambridge. Our late arrival meant that I wasn't able to get a programme, and later ended up paying £15 for one as it was the only programme I needed from matches I had been to.

The 1987-88 season started with another testimonial, again with opposition from the FA Cup Winners, this time Coventry City. Their manager, John Sillett, was one of Hereford's successful managers and was assured of a rousing welcome. The result was a pleasing win, which was followed by further pre-season wins at Gloucester, Evesham and Cheltenham, the last of which we will be playing in the Vauxhall Conference next season. The League season got off to a mixed start, and by the time we lost at Swansea in September, we were bottom of the League. By that stage we had beaten Bristol Rovers in the Littlewoods (League) Cup, and had a prize draw against Nottingham Forest. United had signed Ian Bowyer in the summer, so it was an ideal draw for him. The match as a contest ended at the City ground with a 5-0 defeat, after we had been ripped apart by Franz Carr. By the time the second leg came around, Bowyer had taken over from John Newman, so whether Forest took it easy to give him a better chance of getting the job on a permanent basis is open to question, but the home leg ended 1-1. This season was the only season in which all four Welsh League clubs were in the Fourth Division, but the chance to go to our closest rivals (Newport County) was denied us when the match was switched to a Sunday with away fans banned. The match wasn't all-ticket, however, and by approaching Newport from a different direction, getting into the ground was no problem. Unfortunately, not too many people thought of this, so there was a poor attendance for a poor match, which finished goal-less. We had some consolation by being able to see a 1-0 win at Ninian Park. We had a return visit to Twerton Park in the Freight-Rover and beat Bristol Rovers, although we did qualify for the knockout stages in spite of losing at home to Torquay.

Most of the Hereford fans saw only one FA Cup match this season, although we played two. In the first round we won 1-0 at Barnet, at a time when they were a very good non-league team, and were drawn away to Colchester United in the second round. The experiences of Arsenal having been banished by the free train to Aldershot, another train was organised, with even more disastrous results. Far from arriving at Layer Road after kick-off, British Rail only managed to get us as far as Stratford in East London, where we gave up hope of getting to Colchester and had the idea of going to Orient v Swansea. But the local police had other ideas and we ended up going home without seeing any football whatsoever. From that day to this, Hereford United have not had any special trains to anywhere, in spite of there being several matches when we could have organised them.

Our cup choices were now limited to the Freight-Rover as by this time we had been humiliated by Kidderminster in the Welsh Cup, who left Edgar Street with a 3-0 win. Having beaten Newport 4-2 at home in the League, we played them away in the Freight-Rover, when it became obvious why they had banned our fans from the League match. We won the match 3-2, but then lost 1-0 to Brighton in the Edgar Street mist in the next round. That match was the first time I had seen us lose at home in a competitive match to a team from a higher league. The most notable match of the rest of the season was away at Crewe on Good Friday night. It finished 0-0 and after the match Ian Bowyer came across to the United supporters to thank us for turning up 'in such shitty weather'. It got worse for me as my car (the Citroen had been replaced by a Metro) broke down on the way home!

The 1988-89 season started with a daft idea – a pre-season friendly away at Worcester on a Saturday! The cities are only 24 miles apart, and there is a lot of bitterness in Hereford about spending in the supposed county of Hereford and Worcester staying within a few miles of Worcester, so there has always been fierce rivalry between the two sets of fans and city inhabitants. This manifested itself in yet more fighting in Worcester city centre before the match. A couple of weeks later we made history by being the opposition for Scunthorpe's first League match at Glanford Park, and another new season started with a 3-1 defeat. The League season was notable for its nothingness, with one of the few matches of note being a 4-4 draw with Rochdale, courtesy of another Phil Stant hat-trick.

Our FA Cup run lasted one match, courtesy of a 3-0 defeat against Cardiff City. With City having quite a reputation for violence at Edgar Street, many people would not normally go to Ninian Park, even though trouble there was virtually unknown. However, this was the FA Cup, which is special for United fans, and a reasonable turnout of 800 made the trip. People had heard rumours that some United fans were planning something 'special' for the match, and at half-time it happened. A couple of United fans worked at a plastics factory and had prepared an explosive which activated when coming into contact with liquid, with the result that there was a large explosion in the toilets under the main stand!

With the League being a let-down yet again, it was down to the minor cup competitions to give us some pride. In our Sherpa Van Trophy match at home to Wolves, we controlled the play for most of the match but conceded two unnecessary goals to let Wolves draw 2-2, which proved significant later in the season. A good win at Reading was followed by another one at Colchester, before the area semi-final paired us with Wolves at Edgar Street. Having given them a lifeline in the tournament, they outplayed us to win 2-0 and then went on to beat Burnley 2-0 in the final, which was a sell-out for the first time. The Welsh Cup followed a familiar pattern with an easy win over a 'small' team (Rhos Aelwyd), a good win against a decent team (Newport) and a semi-final defeat against Kidderminster. We lost the away leg 1-0 but the second leg was notable for the fact that Ian Bowyer kept our prolific striker (Phil Stant) on the bench when he was probably the person most likely to score the goal we needed. It was also notable for a duck flying into the ground and proving extremely difficult to shift. Even now many people regard this as the funniest thing they have ever seen at Edgar Street. At the time it was rumoured that Bowyer's decision to keep Stanty on the bench was due to an alleged fall-out they had had at Grimsby the previous Saturday when Stant was substituted.

That day had started with the normal optimism that football fans feel on a Saturday morning. As we drove up alongside the Nottingham Forest fans going to their FA Cup semi-final against Liverpool, we could see them trying to work out whether the black-and-white scarves were of either of their bitterest rivals – Derby or Notts County! Apart from that our journey to the ground was incident-free, but not long after kick-off people with radios said that the FA Cup semi-final had been held up and that there were Liverpool fans on the pitch. I immediately discounted hooliganism as a cause and thought it was more likely that it was down to forged tickets causing overcrowding. There wasn't much more definite news during the match (which was a 1-1 draw), but while we were driving home the full story of what happened at Hillsborough became clear. Even from a distance it was horrific listening and no one could believe what they were hearing. There was certainly a stunned silence in our car, borne out by the fact that none of us spoke until we stopped at Ashby-de-la-Zouch a couple of hours later.

During the course of visiting all 92 League grounds I had been to watch Sheffield Wednesday v Liverpool and stood on the Leppings Lane terraces. Hillsborough made such an impression on me that when I went to the semi-final between Leeds and Coventry at the ground, I made sure of having a seat. It did not come as much of a surprise to me that a disaster like that could happen there, given the layout of the ground and the surrounding areas. While something had to be done about the way football fans were treated and herded into cages, I do think that the Taylor Report was used as an excuse to fleece as much money out of football fans as possible. It also changed the sport's clientele to what it is today. It is a disgrace that football's traditional fan-base has been alienated to the extent that a whole new class of customer has been attracted. Nowadays it seems that people with money are welcomed irrespective of how much they know about the game, as can be seen from the proliferation of executive boxes at grounds and the fact that supporters at Old Trafford have to be encouraged to sing, and possibly risk ejection if they do. There is a definite case for people to have the choice of standing or sitting at matches, as long as it is in safety, before the sport as we know it disappears forever.

The 1989-90 season was the one in which my support for Hereford took on a new dimension. After a couple of seasons when there was no organised travel for supporters, my friend Colin Butler and I decided to do something about it. It involved quite a lot of work but we set up some rules to make it understandable and as inexpensive as possible for the supporters and club officials who sold the tickets for us. The basic rules were that ticket prices were based on the cost of a coach and 30 people travelling, although we would run transport if 25 people had booked. The other premise was that trips tthat made a profit would subsidise those which didn't. One of our first trips was to Charlton Athletic for the second round of the League Cup, which we had reached by beating Torquay United 1-0 and 3-0. After negotiating London's rush hour we arrived at Selhurst Park. Within one minute of kick-off we were 1-0 up through a penalty, but eventually lost 3-1. This was another season when our cup exploits made it all worthwhile.

In the Leyland-DAF Cup we beat Aldershot 3-2 and were sure of progressing to the next round by the time we lost 1-0 to Birmingham City at St Andrew's. In the next round we had a superb win at Peter-borough, but then went out to Notts County on penalties, after miss-ing a penalty during the match. The real excitement was to come in the FA Cup and Welsh Cup. The first round of the FA Cup was away at Farnborough, where a superb day out was had by all. A 1-0 win was only spoilt by the local idiots throwing missiles over the fence at us from outside the ground, and the police threatening to arrest those among us who complained! The second round had us at home to Mer-thyr, where a superb match was won 3-2. After one reasonably local match, we had another in the third round, with Walsall the visitors to Edgar Street. Walsall went 1-0 up and had several chances to sew it up in the last 10 minutes, but somehow we resisted them and scored twice in the last five minutes! The atmosphere when we went 2-1 up was incredible, with the whole home end partying. The partying took on a new dimension 24 hours later with the words, 'Hereford United will play..Manchester United.'

The next week we were home to Cambridge United in the League, and this was rightly made a voucher game for Manchester United tickets. This ensured a crowd of 7302, which when compared to our capacity of just under 14 000, prompted our directors to give Man United 6000 tickets. This did not go down well with the Hereford public as it didn't seem to have been appreciated that some people were unable to get to matches on Saturdays as they either worked or played in local leagues, but that they would have been able to go to the Cup match. By this time, our fanzine *Talking Bull* had appeared, and on the Saturday night before the match (it was a 12 o'clock kick-off on Sunday) the editorial team went out in town selling the next day's issue. The atmosphere was incredibly tense. Quite a few Man United fans were already down for the match, and it seemed that wherever they were, they simply weren't safe. They were even barri-caded in pubs for their own safety!

The match itself was heartbreaking: we gave our all but lost to a goal by Clayton Blackmore in the 85th minute. This was the season when Alex Ferguson was seemingly always one calamitous defeat from being sacked, and that undeserved win was just one in a run that saw United win the Cup. If we had beaten them that day, as we should have done, who knows how English football would have turned out in the past seven years.

By this time we had exorcised our Kidderminster Harriers' ghost with a 3-1 win at Aggborough in the third round of the Welsh Cup. Our celebrations were worthy of having won the Cup, but we had been through varying degrees of hell at their hands over the previous few years! In the quarter-final we were drawn away at Bangor City, but having negotiated the winding roads to North Wales in torrential rain, we arrived just after the match had been called off. Rather than go straight home we went into their Supporters' Club, put 'Daytrip to Bangor' by Fiddlers' Dram on the jukebox and watched Nelson Mandela's release from prison live on TV! The League form had been patchy all season, but there was one memorable weekend spent in Scarborough when a 1-0 win was followed by a glorious night out around Scarborough, and particularly in the Jolly Roger pub. The semi-final of the Welsh Cup was played in the space of three nights, with the first leg at Ninian Park ending in a fantastic 3-0 win for United. Even though we regularly win at Cardiff, we haven't beaten them at Edgar Street since 1976, so we weren't able to relax completely. This became clear as they took a 2-0 lead. Colin Robinson scored but Cardiff went 3-1 up and gave us some anxious moments – another goal would have taken them through on away goals. We held on, though, and were in our first final since 1982.

The opposition was Wrexham and the Welsh FA seemed unable to decide where the match should take place. We would have been quite happy for the match to be played at the Racecourse Ground as it was always a popular away trip for United fans, but we had the next best venue as it became the first Welsh Cup Final to be played at Cardiff Arms Park. United fans turned out in force with 2800 making the trip to Cardiff, in contrast to 800 Wrexham fans. Admittedly they had to travel further and had already qualified for Europe by virtue of the fact that we were ineligible due to being in England, but it was still a pathetic turnout considering it was their Cup Final. In spite of what was at stake, it was an open game with a good atmosphere considering that the crowd of just over 4200 was lost in the magnificent stadium. Colin Robinson put us 1-0 up in the first half but Gary Worthington equalised after half-time. Just when it looked as though the match was going to extra time, the much-maligned Ian Benbow

scored to bring the Cup back to Hereford for the first time. No opportunity was lost and an open-top bus tour around the streets of Hereford was organised a couple of days later!

A couple of weeks before that match, United became the first team
for over 30 years to have a father and son in the same League team
when Ian and Gary Bowyer played in an away match at Scunthorpe.
We came from 3-1 down, with only 10 players and no recognised
striker on the pitch, to draw 3-3. Less than a month after the season
ended, a few of us were having a day out at Porthcawl with our day
dominated by Ian Bowyer's dismissal. The board wanted Ian to sign
Gary on a long contract but father wanted to look after son's best interests, which he saw as being better served at Nottingham Forest. We
could see both sides of the argument, but felt that as the club was paying wages to both of them, the club's interests should take prece-
dence. This situation was a great shame as Bowyer had built the
nucleus of a good team at Edgar Street. The board took a giant leap
back into the past by appointing Colin Addison as his successor. Addison was the club's first League manager, and in spite of having
worked elsewhere (including South Africa and Spain) in the inter-
vening years, had kept a home in Hereford and so was in touch with
events at Edgar Street. He had even had a street named after him in a
housing development near the ground!

Looking back through my records of the 1990-91 season, it is difficult to find much of any significance that happened. One of the most
memorable occurrences was the European Championship qualifying
match between England and the Republic of Ireland at Lansdowne
Road. We organised a coach from Hereford and set off at 8.00pm,
while listening to the commentary of United's Welsh Cup match at
Newtown. When the radio reception gave up the ghost with one
minute remaining, United were 1-0 down, so that wasn't the best start
to our trip. The journey to Fishguard was slow and tortuous, as was
the leg from Rosslare to Dublin. We had a wonderful moment that re-
inforced many people's preconceptions about the Irish people when
the traffic policeman escorting our coach got lost – with us in tow!
Fortunately, there were none of the scenes that caused the abandon-
ment of the 1995 friendly, and the match ended 1-1. We had another
uneventful journey home and arrived home to the news that United
had equalised in the last minute at Newtown and won on penalties!

In February *Talking Bull* became the second fanzine in the country to sponsor a match, and was only beaten to it by a couple of weeks by one of the Millwall fanzines. The match, against Maidstone United, was won 4-0, and the whole day was a proud one for all of us involved with the fanzine. Towards the end of the season I paid a return visit to South Africa for the first time since my departure, and was careful to time it so that I wouldn't miss too much of consequence. Unfortunately, the Welsh Cup semi-final was arranged for my absence, so I missed a visit to the Racecourse Ground for the first time since I started watching United. I was able to make a phone call and find out that it was a 1-1 draw, which was obviously a good result for United. I arrived back in England at 8 on a Friday morning, and the following afternoon was watching United win 2-0 at Ninian Park! That match was followed by the second leg of the Welsh Cup semi-final, but Wrexham beat us 2-1 to reach the final. The season ended with another visit to Scarborough, where the highlight of the match was a 35-minute rendition of 'Colin Addison's Barmy Army', so needless to say we lost.

We had a shock during the close season when Addison decided he had had enough of life back at Edgar Street, probably due to the pressure on him to succeed. So – for the second time – he was followed by John Sillett. As the first manager to lead United to promotion, he immediately had the same pressure on him to repeat the feat, regardless of the fact that we didn't have the players or recent form to make that a likely occurrence. Two of his more memorable signings were Greg Downs, who, of course, had been with him at Coventry City when they won the FA Cup in 1987, and Paul Robinson, whose claim to fame was scoring the winner when Scarborough beat Chelsea in the League Cup.

Our first match of the 1991-92 season was away at Wrexham and a magnificent following of 1100 turned up to cheer United to victory, after Robinson and Joey Jones were sent-off for fighting. We obviously didn't know it at the time, but Robinson would be sent off in two away matches and we won both of them 1-0 (the other was Northampton)! In spite of losing to Barnet in their second home match as a League club, we didn't have a bad start to the season, and when we beat York City 2-1 in mid-September, we went top of the League. Our next match was at Walsall, so at 60 miles away and with us top of the

League, a good turnout was expected, but for United to take 1500 to an away League match was unheard of in my experience. That was where the good times in the League came to an abrupt halt, as the Saddlers hammered us 3-0. The most galling aspect of the match was when Paul McLoughlin, who was Phil Stant's striking partner when they scored 45 goals between them in one season and so liked immensely, scored, he came over to us and milked the moment in no uncertain terms. Events like that, which are not a one-off, make you wonder if players do care in the slightest for the clubs and the fans they play for, or whether to them it is just a job. You can understand if the player concerned has been abused at a club, but when they are popular it leaves a bitter taste in the mouth.

Moving on from there, the sporting calendar that year was dominated by the Rugby World Cup, and on the day of the final at Twickenham we were playing Maidstone at Dartford. That had been quite a popular trip in the short time that we played them, and considering the distance and the counter-attraction of the rugby, a reasonable 150 made the journey. When we went into the ground we could have been forgiven for thinking that it was a reserve match as there were so few people there. The match started well as United soon went 2-0 up, but Maidstone fought back to 2-2 before one of those moments you hope will never happen to your team, does. Maidstone's goalkeeper, Ian Hesford, kicked the ball downfield and one bounce later it was over Tony Elliott's head and in the back of our net. Luckily, there weren't many people there to see it, as the inflated-looking attendance of 846 confirmed! Our FA Cup exploits began with a visit to Atherstone United, where one of our drinking acquaintances lived for a while, so he recommended a pub for us to meet in. At this time, as well as organising the official club transport, I would occasionally run a minibus for some friends and myself, and this was the ideal opportunity. The people on the minibus would invariably be run-of-the-mill, peaceful supporters who liked a few pints and a meal before the match, and today was no exception. We arrived in Atherstone at about 11.30am and parked the minibus opposite the railway station, which was near the recommended pub. For the first hour it was great as we had a quiet drink and some food, but we noticed the pub filling up with what didn't take a rocket-scientist to work out was their mob. Not wanting any trouble, we left and went elsewhere, but the bush telegraph was in operation and the same thing happened in the next pub. Luckily, there were a couple of sensible Atherstone fans in there who had sussed out what was going on and gave us a lift to the ground. We found out that it had been kicking-off at all the pubs near the ground, but the match itself was trouble-free, apart from when the Portaloo in the away end threatened to slide down the precarious muddy bank it was perched on! The match ended in a 0-0 draw so it meant that we hadn't been humiliated on the pitch, although it was unpleasant enough off it. On the way back to the minibus things got really nasty with missiles being thrown across the main street in the town centre by the assorted idiots. When we finally reached the mini-bus, we couldn't help noticing that it had several windows missing. On reporting this to the police, we were given the helpful, 'Well I'm sure you'll do it to theirs in the replay.' Not wanting to stoop to their level, we didn't do anything to them or any of their minibuses, although matters were helped by the team winning the replay 3-0.

The week before the second round saw one of our greatest humiliations as Maesteg Park came to Edgar Street in the Welsh Cup and won 2-1, which didn't do people's confidence much good for the visit to Aylesbury. Consequently, there was a very poor turnout of about 500, but the labours of (Cliff) Hercules were not enough to stop us winning 3-2. The third round gave us yet another away trip to a non-league club, with Woking the destination for our travelling support and one of my mini-buses. Due to a combination of too many people buying me drinks and not having enough time to drink them at a comfortable pace, I ended up decorating the pavement outside the pub, but luckily I was back to normal by the time we got to the ground. This match was played at a time when, like now, Woking were developing a reputation as being a very good non-league team, and it seemed as though our team's main strategy was not to concede any goals and to finish them off in a replay. The only time this looked like not working was when Steve 'Woody' Devine cleared off the line with the rest of the team beaten, and the value of the day's efforts became clear when a trip to Nottingham Forest awaited the winners of the replay. With such a big prize on offer, over 8000 packed into Edgar Street, and our experience saw us to a 2-1 win. This was the first time it occurred to me that my decision to organise the club's away travel might not have been a sensible one, as Herefordshire went cup-crazy yet again. Luckily, the match was scheduled for a Sunday, when normal bus services were at a premium, because otherwise I don't think our carriers, the biggest in the county, would have coped! The official club travel alone numbered 18 coaches, and by the time all the pubs had organised their own (plus mine – no mere minibus today!) there were 52 coachloads of Hereford United supporters en route to the City Ground. Our only regret was that ours was the only match in the area, so there weren't any other supporters on the motorways to be impressed by the size of our travelling support. This match also saw the biggest disaster that *Talking Bull* has associated itself with – the special souvenir T-shirts. We took in the interest around the county, the high profile of John Sillett and a Monty Python sketch, and designed a T-shirt showing Sillett chopping down a tree (as featured on the Forest badge) with the words 'I'm a lumberjack and I'm OK'. We thought they would sell like hot cakes, but they simply bombed and we ended up giving them away to the Junior Bulls!

The match was one-way traffic as Forest tore us apart, but only clinched the victory with a second goal, in the last minute, when Teddy Sheringham added to Stuart Pearce's first-half goal. However, we did have chances which, if they had fallen to strikers instead of inexperienced midfielders, could have seen a very undeserved upset. One of my greatest memories of following Hereford came after the match when our coaches were waiting to be escorted out of Nottingham. Our coach was in the middle of the queue, and as we went round a roundabout all you could see in either direction was Hereford coaches and minibuses taking 6500 supporters home.

The rest of the season was notable only for the home match against Walsall on Easter Saturday, when the disillusionment with the way the club was drifting aimlessly, with no obvious sense of purpose, manifested itself in a red-card protest against the directors. It was peaceful and had the effect that the Supporters' Club Chairman and organiser of the protest, Keith Benjamin, was elected to the board as an associate director. The season ended on a very high note for me as my first love, Leeds United, won the First Division against the odds stacked in favour of the forces of evil, Manchester United, which made it all the more sweet. Any chance of continuity within Hereford came to nothing when history repeated itself and John Sillett decided that being Central TV's expert summariser was preferable to trying to revive our fortunes, with the result that Greg Downs was promoted to manager.

Once again an early match saw us entertain Manchester United in a testimonial. In anticipation of a big crowd we printed extra copies of *Talking Bull*, but in the week before the match it was leaked out that the Manchester United first team was on tour in Scandinavia. The team to come to Edgar Street would consist of fringe first-team players, with the balance made up by the youth team. Unfortunately, the match programme doesn't help to solve the problem of who actually played for Manchester United that day as it lists the first team squad, but it is possible that United fans saw the likes of David Beckham, Nicky Butt, Paul Scholes and Gary and Philip Neville earlier than most football supporters!

The most notable event of the season occurred on Sunday, 6th September when United played Northampton Town at the County Ground. The referee was Brian Coddington, who had previously sent three Newcastle United players off in a match at Derby, and incurred the wrath of Kevin Keegan in the process. He excelled himself this time by sending off four of our players in a truly bizarre display of refereeing, which really did defy belief at times. What made it even more remarkable was that we drew 1-1, with our goal coming when we were already down to nine men! For the first time since I had started watching Hereford I chose not to go to a FA Cup match. I had tickets for England v South Africa at Twickenham instead. But United succeeded where Coventry City had failed with a 2-1 win against Sutton United at Gander Green Lane. The second round was against familiar opponents but at an unfamiliar ground – Yeovil Town had moved from the old, sloping Huish to a new Huish further from the town centre. 1700 United fans made the trip south. Due to the antics of a few idiots, many had to watch the second half with a line of policemen and horses obscuring our view of the pitch, which didn't exactly do wonders for the humour of those who do know how to behave at a football match. The match ended goal-less and another large attendance at a midweek replay was guaranteed by a home tie against Arsenal for the winners. Unfortunately, United contrived to commit football and financial suicide by losing 2-1, with Greg Downs not setting the best of examples by being sent off. For those of us who had been following United for ten years or less, this was the first time we had known defeat by a non-league club in the FA Cup, but unfortunately it was an experience we would grow horribly accustomed to in the next two years.

We didn't even have much in the Autoglass Trophy to look forward to as an abysmal performance on a miserable night saw us lose 4-0 to Northampton – what was it about the County Ground and the number '4' that season? By now we were becoming an integral part of the battle to avoid relegation, but a determined run from the end of March resulted in only one defeat in our last nine matches, and that in a match when our safety had already been ensured. The most amazing of these matches was away at Crewe Alexandra, who as usual were pushing for promotion and playing very good football in the process. They tore us apart for virtually the entire 90 minutes and we could not have complained if we had been beaten 10-0, but as it was Crewe scored their equaliser with 15 minutes to go. We had got off lightly and we knew it, but would pay for it the following season. With three weekends of the season remaining, four clubs were in danger of relegation – Torquay United, Northampton Town, Halifax Town and ourselves, but when we went to Torquay we knew that one point would be enough for us as the others had to play each other. Another fine display got us a 0-0 draw but we were unable to celebrate with the players due to Torquay's new-found hooligan fringe invading the pitch. However, we made up for that in no uncertain terms by taking over one of the pubs in the centre of Torquay for the night, with the celebrations taking on a new dimension when we heard that our youth team had won the Welsh Cup that afternoon!

Defeat in a low-key match against Doncaster Rovers was irrelevant, but the final match assumed nationwide importance as we had to travel to Halifax, who needed to beat us and hope that Shrewsbury beat Northampton in order to avoid relegation. For all the state of disrepair that The Shay (the ground) was failing into, The Shay Hotel and other hostelries in the town meant that Halifax was our preference to stay up, and if that meant us losing, so be it. We had already decided to take a leaf out of West Brom's supporters' book by having a theme of a beachwear party for the day, so it was a motley crew that was touring the pubs of Halifax for about three hours prior to the match. Once in the ground, the inflatable crocodiles and sharks were making their presence felt, but disaster struck in the first half when

Derek Hall scored for United. He used to play for Halifax and his dejected stroll back to the halfway line was reminiscent of Denis Law on that glorious day when his backheeled goal sent Manchester United into the Second Division. There was still hope as Shrewsbury were 2-0 up, but Hereford fans know Shrewsbury cannot be relied on when you need them, and Northampton came back to win 3-2, which at least absolved us of sole responsibility for Halifax's demise. The prospect of another trip to West Yorkshire is one of the more appetising in our forthcoming season in the Conference.

The 1993-94 season started disastrously with defeats in the first four matches, the fourth of which was a 4-3 thriller at home to Wycombe Wanderers, who had just been promoted from the Conference. With the fifth match being away to Scunthorpe United, it was difficult to see when our luck would change, but a superb performance saw us off the mark with a 2-1 win. The season really took off in terms of excitement in September and October, when a 3-0 win at home to Wigan Athletic was followed by a 1-0 win against Walsall in the Autoglass Trophy, the first time we had beaten them since our FA Cup win in January 1990. The following Saturday we played the Saddlers again, this time at the Bescot Stadium, and saw an exciting 3-3 draw, which prompted the caption on the next issue of *Talking Bull* to read, 'Nice forward line, shame about the defence.'

Following on from a win against our traditional Coca-Cola Cup opponents, Torquay United, in the first round, we entertained Premiership opposition in the awkward shape of Wimbledon. We realised that this tie would give us a rare chance to have a bigger attendance for our home game than our opponents would have for theirs. Considering their status, we actually achieved it with ease – our 4872 being more than double their 2151 (including 400 United supporters at Selhurst Park!). We were predictably beaten 5-1 on aggregate. The next match saw Crewe get revenge for their wastefulness in front of goal the previous season as they equalled our biggest ever League defeat by beating us 6-0. The following week we beat Colchester United 5-0, with Chris Pike scoring each goal of his hat-trick past a different goalkeeper! In between these two matches there was another trip to watch England play abroad. The infamous match at Rotterdam did as much as anything to bring Graham Taylor's reign as England manager to an end, although it has to be said that events did conspire against him on the night.

With our League form continuing to rise occasionally and fall regularly, highlights were few and far between, and a 0-5 home defeat by Chester City signalled a post-match demonstration against anyone and everyone in authority. The FA Cup brought one of our greatest humiliations. After an abysmal match at Cambridge City in the first round, we lost 2-1 away at Bath City in the second, with the match shown live on Sky. We were the better side on balance of play, but that counted for nothing in the end. Once again the main plus was our support and we sold out the away terrace at Twerton Park.

Three weeks later my life was to change forever when I met up with a girl called Zena, who I had met on holiday a few months earlier. We started going out together, and in spite of (or probably because of!) several exposures to Hereford United, I have not been able to transmit my love for the beautiful game to her. Nevertheless, we are now married and have now increased our family. Although Hereford United are a very important part of my life and have the capacity for making me very happy, they also have a tendency to let me down as often if not more, which is not something I could accuse Zena of doing. The start of our romance inevitably led to different choices having to be made. Consequently, in the time since 2nd January 1994, my attendance at United matches has not been as regular as before. The main moment of note in the remainder of that season almost inevitably involved a match against Northampton Town, who we always seem to play in matches of great importance. Not for the first time, both clubs were near the bottom of the League, and although there were still two months of the season to go, this match was identified as being of particular significance. We hyped up the match in the fanzine and the local press, and persuaded the club to agree to make up any shortfall on the cost of coaches to allow a reduction in prices. In the end this wasn't necessary as all coaches were filled, and the best part of 1000 fans, in the division's biggest crowd of the day, cheered United on to a 1-0 win.

My life changed again at the beginning of April when, after a long illness, my father passed away. It could not have been timed for a worse day as it was the day when United were away at Shrewsbury Town in the local derby, but there was no way I could have gone to the match in my frame of mind that day. So, Bill Shankly, football is very important to many people, but not that important.

The 1994-95 season started with Greg Downs still in charge, but few people could have envisaged just how ironically his tenure would come to an end. The League season had seen its usual shaky start with another eccentric display of refereeing prominent in an early match at Scarborough. United had gone into the match with one point but no goals from the first three matches, as well as a goal-less draw at home to West Bromwich Albion in the Coca-Cola Cup. It was at this point that we first became aware of a new referee on the League list – Uriah Rennie of Sheffield. We managed to score in this match but lost 3-1, mainly due to the fact that we played a fair part of the match with nine players. If my memory serves me correctly one of the dismissals was for two bookable offences, which is fair enough, but our goalkeeper was sent off for a foul committed about 10 yards from the goal line, but virtually on the touchline. Quite how Mr Rennie saw fit to think that it was a clear goalscoring opportunity and thus a professional foul is a mystery to me, but it's typical of the lack of consistency shown by referees in the game today. In the same fixture this past season, John Williams was brought down by a rugby tackle when through on goal, and the offender wasn't even booked!

Going back to 1994, United claimed one of the greatest victories in our history with a 1-0 win at the Hawthorns in the second leg of the Coca-Cola cup-tie. As in the previous ten years, I worked for the club sponsors of the time, Sun Valley Poultry, and was not best pleased when I wasn't able to get any time off work to go to the match. In between the Scarborough and West Bromwich matches, United had won 3-1 at Rochdale, so it was quite a surprise that Downs was sacked within a week. John Layton, who like his father before him was Hereford through and through, was promoted to manager and took charge of the team for a 3-0 defeat at Doncaster. His second game in charge was yet another cup-tie at Nottingham Forest, when we shocked all and sundry by going 1-0 up before someone called Stan Collymore scored twice. In the last minute Chris Pike had an excellent chance to equalise but rolled the ball just past the post. With the second leg ending 0-0, that could well have been another momentous giant killing in our list. Instead another giant killing (relatively speaking) was just around the corner. At home to Hitchin Town in the first round of the FA Cup, we were 2-0 down at half-time, but came back well in the second half to draw 2-2. Unfortunately, the replay was no better and we deservedly went down 4-2. Comfortable wins followed against Northampton in the League and Peterborough in the Auto-Windscreens Shield before we entered the amazing Christmas period.

In the last match before Christmas we outplayed Walsall but lost 4-3, on Boxing Day we suffered the heaviest defeat in our history when Mansfield Town beat us 7-1. On the following day a revamped team outplayed Exeter 3-0. At the end of January we made the short trip to St Andrews for the Auto-Windscreens match against Birmingham City, at a time when they were reducing prices for such matches. In filthy weather, a crowd of 22 000 saw the Blues' class tell as they beat us 3-1 in a good match. There were fears of how the likes of the Zulus might react to visiting support in excess of 800, but in the end the only problems we had were with the West Midlands Police. The section of the ground given to away fans was in front of the executive boxes and as it rained incessantly throughout the match, United fans had to stand to avoid sitting on the wet seats. This upset the corporate customers behind to the extent that the police threatened to arrest all the Hereford fans, but in the end had to be content with snatch squads. With our League status safe long before the end, the season petered out towards the close.

During the summer there were rumblings of discontent concerning John Layton's position as manager, and without going into all the claims and counter-claims, his tenure came to an end in slightly acrimonious circumstances. This was a pity as he is a Hereford United man at heart, but there is no room for sentiment among the dead men of football, and the time came to look for a new manager. A mere 21 months after it was suggested in the fanzine that he might be a good choice for United's manager, Graham Turner was appointed to succeed Layton! He didn't have much time to get to know the players he had inherited before the season started, which made the events of the 1995-96 season all the more remarkable. The season started with a 4-1 win against Barnet, including a goal direct from a kick downfield by our goalkeeper, Chris MacKenzie. To the best of our knowledge this makes United the only team to be on the giving and receiving end of one of these rare occurrences!

The saddest event of the season happened in the early hours of Sunday, 1st October, when our Supporters' Club was destroyed in what was later found to be an arson attack. As its name suggests, it was the focal point of the pre- and post-match entertainment, where home and away fans could meet and have a drink together. Although another room at the club has since been given over to the same use, it simply isn't the same, and its loss is still mourned. The League season drifted along much the same as previous ones had, with the highlight once again being the FA Cup. The first round saw us at home to Stevenage Borough and winning 2-1 in a close match, while Sutton United were beaten 2-0 in the second round. This brought about our first appearance in the third round since 1992, and we were rewarded with one of the best possible draws – Tottenham Hotspur at home.

There were mutterings that the club might take the money and run by switching the match to White Hart Lane, due to Edgar Street having a capacity of only 8800. Fortunately this temptation was resisted and the latest in a line of glamour clubs had to come to Edgar Street, followed closely by hordes of journalists and TV crews on the trail of an upset. In truth they should have had one. Ronnie Rosenthal put Spurs 1-0 up when he got in the way of a Darren Caskey shot that was going hopelessly wide and diverted it into the net. We had a glorious chance to equalise in the second half when we were awarded a penalty, but Dean Smith put the ball into the United fans behind Ian Walker's goal. Luckily, this didn't prove too costly as John Brough equalised from a corner a couple of minutes later. The rest of the match was all United but we couldn't get the winner and had to settle for receipts from a sell-out crowd in the replay! Once again you realised the potential at Edgar Street (if only someone could give us a successful team) when 4500 fans packed into the away end and outsang the home support for 90 minutes, in spite of being hammered 5-1. The period after the match finished was one that will stay in my memory a very long time – a raucous rendition of 'Graham Turner's Barmy Army' rang around the ground for 15 minutes!

By this time we had also qualified for the Southern Semi-Finals of the Auto Windscreen Shield, where our opponents were Shrewsbury Town at Gay Meadow. Many of the 1500 United fans who travelled up the A49 remarked how the fields of Herefordshire were covered in snow, but those of Shropshire weren't, until we realised that all the snow in Shropshire was on the pitch! United didn't adjust well to the conditions and were beaten 4-1 in a disappointing performance. This now left us to concentrate on the League, which was in some need of concentration. At the start of March there were ten Saturdays of the season remaining, but we still had 17 matches to play. With a small squad and limited resources, that is fixture congestion, Mr Ferguson, not when you have to play those matches and have about 9 internationals in the reserves! The situation was such that if we won all our matches in hand we would be in the play-offs, but if we started getting injuries and lost a few games, we would get sucked into the danger zone.

Our first match in March marked the return from injury of Tony James, who had been injured in the 7-1 record defeat at Mansfield 14 months earlier. In a scene that would have been rejected as being too far-fetched for *Roy of the Rovers*, James went upfield for a corner in the last minute and scored the only goal of the match. That match was the start of a run that, although it included a couple of defeats, took us into the play-offs for the only time in our history. Unfortunately, there wasn't a happy ending as we lost in both legs to Darlington.

The encouraging end to the season meant that optimism was at an all-time high for the start of the 1996-97 season, until three of the club's most influential players left during the summer of 1996. Richard Wilkins had gone to Colchester, but the two moves that really rankled were Steve White and Tony James, who went to Cardiff and Plymouth respectively. White had scored 32 goals the previous season, but wanted a two-year contract while we were prepared to offer only a one-year deal to a 38-year-old striker. Obviously it was galling to see him move to our local rivals, but only this coming year will tell whether our judgement was correct.

In a feature in a national magazine several other fanzine editors predicted us to win the League, but the upheavals of the summer led me to think that mid-table would be the best we could hope for. As events subsequently showed, even that was hopelessly optimistic. The season never really got going for us, with very few sequences of more than two wins or defeats all season. The most notable match prior to the last match of the season was our away leg in the Coca-Cola Cup second round, when Middlesbrough's talented array of foreigners tore us apart to give us our biggest ever defeat (7-0), with Fabrizio Ravanelli scoring four times. The second leg was obviously never going to be a contest, and while we didn't expect Middlesbrough to send their full first team, we were still looking forward to seeing a couple of their best-known stars. In the end we had to be content with Branco and Mikkel Beck. No disrespect to these two players or any others who made the journey, but the crowd-pullers were definitely Ravanelli, Emerson and the brilliant Juninho. Prior to that night I had a lot of respect for Bryan Robson and all that he had achieved in the game, but he lost a lot of that with his comment that he did not have an obligation to entertain the Hereford public. Middlesbrough's subsequent relegation as a result of not fielding a team against Blackburn was therefore not a cause for widespread mourning among Hereford supporters.

The season limped along from that time, and as it became clear that we were in serious trouble, it always seemed likely that Brighton were going to have what was necessary to close the gap between them and us. In spite of what people may have said, we still felt that most preferred us to be relegated rather than Brighton, as they have the potential and, therefore, the support to bring revenue to all the other clubs in the division. We were proud of our team and the way we went for a win in the last match, but despite having a lot of chances it was not to be our day, and our 25-year stay in the League ended with a lot of tears. We are merely flirting with a return.

While I still, and always will, retain my affection for Leeds United, I now regard myself as a Hereford United fan first and foremost. One of the highlights of following a club like Hereford is the camaraderie from the social side of the game, when you meet up with a group of people from all over the country who all have the same interest. We generally meet up for a meal and a few drinks, whether at The Victory in Hereford, The Cemetery in Rochdale or any number of watering holes in any other town with a League or non-league team! We have absolutely no interest in violence – only having a good time watching our team and meeting up with the opposition supporters if possible. The future is definitely uncertain. We feel that we need an excellent season in 1998-99, with promotion back into the Football League essential. If this happens, relegation might just have been acceptable (if not pleasant!) as it could give us new-found belief in our team. If we don't bounce straight back we are pessimistic for the future of Hereford United, and for many people, life without our team just won't be the same.

Chapter 9

Do the Ayatollah!
Phil Stead aka Eric the Red

*From Lincoln City and too much cider to Edgar
Street and lost false teeth.*

It's the apples that does it. You can drink bitter all day long and you'll just fall asleep. You can go both ways with lager. But when you start on the apples, you're admitting to yourself that you want to lose control. And we started early that morning.

It had been a great night. We went to Chapter Arts Centre in Canton to see our mates in a band, U Thant. Two of the band have gone on to greater things. The bass player is in Catatonia, and one of the guitarists plays with the Super Furry Animals. But the man who has contributed most to Welsh culture is the singer, Rhys. He created the Ayatollah.

Rhys was watching the news on Friday night and witnessed the incredible scenes at the Ayatollah Khomeni's funeral in Iran. Thousands of Iranians were beating themselves about the heads, many with rocks, as their grievance took the form of self-inflicted pain. Looks like fun, thought Rhys, and that Friday night we were all 'doing the Ayatollah' as we danced on stage, naked but for empty tomato crates.

The van pulled up at 6am for the long trip to Lincoln. It's even longer when there are thirteen of you in the back of a fishmonger's van with nothing to sit on. I was on the cider by nine. With a tedious 0-0 draw on the pitch, you have to make your own entertainment. So with 20 minutes left, the City terracing hosted a cider-fuelled rave. Enter the criminal intelligence film crew, yeah, actual 'spotters'. What NCIS thought they were going to gain by filming the two coachloads from the supporters' club and a fish van full of students, I don't know. What they got was a clothed version of last night's gig. It was hard work but eventually the rest of the City fans caught on, and by the end there were 120 'doing the Ayatollah'.

As luck would have it, the following week took us to Hereford, always a big attraction for the nutters. And there were 4000 there! Mainly because Chairman Rick Wright failed to get the match moved from the Sunday and told Hereford that all Cardiff fans would now boycott the fixture. Did we hell as like.

I went to the match with a bloke who is now an agent to many of the Welsh professionals. We had a few pub-stops, and at the last one I downed a pint a bit too quickly and 'felt unwell' in a hedge. It was only when I got to the match I realised I had lost my new false teeth, which I gave up as a bad job. I'd just got in when I saw people from the Lincoln match and they started doing the Ayatollah. There's a nice, flat terrace at Hereford where nobody stands because you can't see the pitch. If you run up and down there slapping your head for half an hour, you soon get noticed. I heard some people whispering that I was from Kent. At least that's what it sounded like.

But people like it, and after the match a whole train of cars headed back to South Wales full of Valleys Commandos leaning out of the windows and even roof-surfing, slapping their heads at the same time. My own day out was saved when I found my teeth in the hedge. A quick swill and they were back in.

The Ayatollah routine was seen at most away games that season, 1991-92, and the final game at Peterborough was designated an Ayatollah Fancy Dress Party. So it was that 1500 blokes with tea towels on their heads headed for London Road. It was fun following Cardiff in those days and I was pleased to come 456th in the Ayatollah cross-terrace dash. A senior police officer was congratulating me on the behaviour of the City fans, and apologising for expecting trouble when we saw that 30 nutters were on the pitch and trying to get the ball off Posh's tricky right-winger. He left them trailing and slotted the ball home. To everyone's astonishment, City got what they deserved and the referee allowed the goal.

The Ayatollah moved on from being a daft terrace routine and became a fully-fledged craze in 1993. Coinciding with City's most successful season in years, the media caught on and Sky's coverage of the Autoglass Trophy derby took the Ayatollah to a national audience, as did the BBC's live showing of the Manchester City cup-tie. TV and radio commentators discussed the phenomenon and the *Wales on Sunday* ran a full page with absurd computerised graphics showing readers how to 'do the Ayatollah'. *The South Wales Echo* ran a photo series of people doing the Ayatollah in different parts of the world. A terrified-looking Ryan Giggs was pictured in Corfu with his hands on his head.

The best Ayatollah performance ever came to Scunthorpe of all places. City were already promoted from Division 3 and we took over 5000 to Scunnie's brand new Meccano Stadium. Tickets were in so much demand that we were given three sides of the ground, including Scunthorpe's home end. Scunthorpe didn't dare win and we cruised to a 3-0 victory. It was a strange feeling to see thousands of people in the far north-east slapping their heads, and to think back to

It's there! Jon Coates of Swansea City equalises against rivals Cardiff City at the Vetch Field in 1998. In the background is David Ronney, who played for both clubs.

the Ayatollah's modest beginnings in front of less than 50 in Chapter Arts Centre.

The highlight of my career as a fan, if not the highlight of my life, came with a Wales friendly against Brazil at the Arms Park. I happen to be a sousaphone player and was an occasional member of a Cardiff street band. When I was told that the band were to perform on the pitch for the match, I took my chance. Bugger the sousa playing, I was doing the Ayatollah in the centre circle in front of 30 000 – I was playing for Wales at the Arms Park. That brought my first brush with the law. I had to audition in front of a panel of bobbies to prove that I could, in fact, play the instrument and wasn't just a drunken head-slapper. Which I was. But I could.

The second brush with the law was a bit more serious. When Chris Pike put Cardiff 1-0 up at the Vetch in the Welsh Cup, I celebrated by standing on a crash barrier and doing the Ayatollah. A snatch squad brushed aside the threat of my female companion and took me away. At first I though they were joking, especially when I was led to the cells underneath the North Bank and heard some coppers protesting. 'You can't nick him, he was doing the Ayatollah at the Brazil game.' This was followed by a chant of, 'He ain't done nothing.' The arresting officer had some trouble explaining the reason for arrest and eventually settled for the heinous crime of 'leading the singing'. I was detained until midnight and released without charge after they studied the video evidence.

The Ayatollah routine has now become more of a badge of faith. It's the first thing that City fans do when they meet other City fans in unexpected places. Like pubs. And away games. New players are expected to pay their respects and slap their heads as soon as they step on the pitch for their debut. Performed by City fans for all sorts of things away from the ground, the Ayatollah is moving on from football and can often be seen at big Cardiff gigs in an ironic move back to its roots. It is strange to think that it's been going on now for over seven years, and even stranger to see young kids slapping their heads in the Canton Stand who have probably got no idea whey they are doing it. Then again, neither have I. I just know that it was the apples that did it.

Chapter 10

The Red, Red Robin of London Town

Peter Williams

*Believe it or not, Wales has three teams. Wrexham
FC are the first!*

No one chooses to support a team like Wrexham: it's an accident of
circumstances. You do it because you were born or grew up there, or
because your dad takes you along when you're little and you get
hooked. Or because you're Welsh and there's no one else in North
Wales to support and you're not one of those misguided enough to
cross the English border in search of fulfilment. As at every football
club, the majority of Wrexham fans go when they feel like it, when the
team is having a good run or if there's a cup-tie against a big team. But
Wrexham, like every football club, also has its dedicated followers,
typically strong-minded and loyal, but perhaps more inclined than
most to stand their ground. Maybe it's because we feel under threat
from the English, less than five miles away, and our fellow Welshmen
to the south. It's true to say that, for the Wrexham fan, footballing ad-
versaries come in many guises:

- There are the nearby Merseyside and Manchester clubs who for
  many years have enticed weak-willed young supporters away
  from the town with the prospect of big-time success.

- There are the English. In spite of (or, more likely, because of) their
  closeness to the border, Wrexham fans are proud of their Welsh-
  ness and pass up no opportunity to proclaim it loudly on the terraces, especially in seasons when Wrexham are the highest
  placed Welsh club and the sole fliers of the Welsh dragon in their
  division.

■ Sorry if you're a South Walian reading this, but the fact is that a fair amount of animosity has grown over the years towards South Wales in general and Cardiff in particular. Wrexham fans feel harshly treated both by BBC Wales, who they feel give greater coverage to clubs from South Wales, and by the Welsh FA, who now prefer Cardiff as the location both for their own offices and for international matches.

■ Finally, there's Chester, our traditional local rivals and the objects of scorn rather than animosity, at least in recent times. All you need to know about the inhabitants of Chester is that, out of all the people in the world, it was Gyles Brandreth they elected to represent them in the House of Commons.

I have supported Wrexham since the day in April 1970 when my dad took me along to watch the team win promotion to the Third Division under the captaincy of Eddie May. (Funny how ideas change: in those days he was probably the most popular player at the Racecourse.

Wrexham FC "when trophies were inevitable"

Now, after some unnecessarily malicious jibes in our direction when he was in charge at Cardiff – that North/South divide again! – he is held in contempt by all Wrexham fans.)

I watched Albert Kinsey (what a name!) score our first goal in Europe, was convinced as anyone else that we would win promotion in 1976/77 and then dejected as anyone else when we failed to do so. We finally did it in style the following season with what was the best Wrexham team I have seen (so far!).

In those days, I had always been used to dragging myself away from 'Grandstand' or 'World of Sport' (whatever happened to Dickie Davies and Fred Dineage?) at 2.15 on a Saturday afternoon and arriving at my place on the Racecourse terraces before five to three. In the early 1980s, though, the search for full-time employment forced me across the border and south to London. Until then a prime example of the typical Wrexham obsessive I have described, I now took on an additional set of problems and frustrations: those of the exiled supporter. These are shared, I know, by a large number of Wrexham fans I have met at and outside grounds all over the country.

When I arrived in London, I suddenly had to put a lot more thought and planning into my football outings. Instead of a twenty-minute walk to the ground, I now depended on a Network South East Railcard to get me there. Towards the end of each season, I developed an unhealthy interest in the fates of teams like Orient, Fulham and Oxford, hoping that promotion or relegation would force them into Wrexham's division and offer me an extra chance to see my team play. Since moving to London, I have been obliged to travel a ridiculous number of times to some desperate footballing outposts, grounds which I would surely otherwise have visited only once or twice – godforsaken places like the Abbey Stadium, Cambridge and London Road, Peterborough, the latter the scene of some of the most woeful Wrexham performances in recent years. The dreadful 3-1 defeat in the 1989-90, the season we all but lost our place in the League, stands out particularly in my memory. I remember Joey Jones coming on as substitute, being booked for his first tackle and sent off for his second, staying on the field of play for about five minutes in all.

Trips to Peterborough have always ended in defeat, normally 1-0 after we've dominated the play for 85 minutes. Anyone who has suffered as I have at London Road will have no doubt that the 1996-7 4-2 victory there was the highlight of our cup run. For two weeks and two fantastic cup-ties, Kevin Russell suddenly rediscovered the art of goalscoring – at the time of writing, those were the last goals he scored! But if his two cracking strikes that Tuesday evening in February mean that the London Road bogey has finally been laid to rest, we will forgive him for not having a goalscoring opportunity since.

Anyone who's followed the team away from home for any length of time will have seen plenty of defeats, but some of my Wrexham FC away days ended in failure before I even got anywhere near the ground. In 1990 my brother and I sat in a ten-mile tailback on the eastern side of the Severn Bridge, finally arriving in Cardiff, where Wrexham had a 7.30 kick-off, at half past nine. A few years later, the car broke down half an hour before a Saturday kick-off at the Racecourse. Having had no problem with the M1, M6 and M54, it finally decided that it was being driven just **too close** to Chester for comfort and gave up the ghost. We waited an hour and a half for a lift the ten or so miles to Wrexham!

One of the problems of anyone unable to get to games is that of finding out the result. Thankfully, since teletext has become widely available much of the strife in this respect has been eliminated. But if, like me, you don't have the luxury of teletext and you live outside the range of the radio coverage of Marcher Sound and Radio 4 Wales, here are a few measures I've resorted to in the past in an effort to find out that crucial final score:

1. Tune into the Sports/Football programme on Radio Five – midweek coverage is patchy. You invariably have to sit through reports on Premier League games (fair enough) and, more frustratingly, results of Division One non-entities before getting to the important news. At least on a Saturday the Sports Report format is reassuringly familiar: scores as they come in at fifteen or ten minutes to five (although why is it that the Wrexham fixture is invariably one of the last ones through?), followed by James Alexander Gordon after the five o'clock news and sporting headlines. There are advantages in the reliably unchanging order of things on Sports Report. Once, while eating in a West End restaurant, I was able to tune in at exactly the right moment to hear an important result from Bootham Crescent, York, although I

did have considerable trouble explaining to my fellow-diners how absolutely essential it was that I did this.

2. You can listen to the match commentary on ClubCall, although anyone who has paid premium charges on their phone bill for listening to its tortuously drawn-out match reports – not to mention the pearls of wisdom of Mr Kevin Reeves (our assistant manager, allegedly, what **else** does he do for his money?) – will realise that this is a non-starter. You can ring up for the result afterwards of course, but there's always the possibility that you'll call too early and get yesterday's message anyway, giving you the team news and prospects for the game which has just ended. One time that ClubCall admittedly did come up with the goods for me was when an FA Cup replay against Hull City a couple of years ago went into injury time. The Radio Five programme (Trevor Brooking's 'Football Night' or some such) had already ended when the match went to penalties. With the possibility of a lucrative cup run in the offing if we won and no other means at my disposal, I reached out for the 0891 buttons in perfect time to hear Brian Hughes step up to take and convert the final penalty which put us through. Our lucrative cup run didn't quite materialise, however: we eventually went out in the third round... to Peterborough!

3. You can buy a newspaper the following morning. This is clearly very unsatisfactory as it involves a restless night, an unseemly struggle to open a newspaper in a crowded newsagent's or, even worse, on an even more crowded tube train.

For anyone like me who gets free Internet access at work, the WFC mailing list is an absolute godsend to the exiled fan. It's a shame that I can't get to it quickly enough (i.e. at 4.50 on Saturdays and at 9.20 on Tuesday nights) for it to be a useful emergency source for results, but it is good for match reports, transfer gossip and is an excellent way of venting your frustrations at the latest poor performance by the team. It allows you to keep sane during the close season by having the sort of conversations you'd normally have down the pub after a game. Recent discussions have included:

■ Who's in your worst ever Wrexham eleven? Mine is as follows (go on, indulge me): Ken Hughes, Frankie Jones (sorry Joey!), Bob

Scott, Scott Williams (see also below), Seamus Heath, Ian Arkwright, Sean Reck, Mark Taylor, Paul Emson, Steve Massey and Ollie Kearns – there are plenty of contenders when you think about it, especially for the goalkeeping jersey!

■ Have you ever had a brush with fame by meeting Wrexham stars of the past or present? Although these have sometimes tended to be along the lines of, 'My mate's girlfriend used to go out with the bloke who delivers Gareth Owen's milk and apparently he's a right miserable bastard.' (He isn't by the way. At least, not as far as I know.)

■ Reserve full-back Scott Williams, er, he's crap, isn't he? (Yes, we decided, he is crap!)

More than a hundred of us now subscribe to the mailing list, mostly exiled North Walians, many living in the UK, but some abroad as well. A friend who joined the list when she recently moved from Reading to Azerbaijan says she's never been so well up on club news!

I am convinced that there is a breed of Wrexham season ticket holder who hates watching the team. Year after year they stand on the terraces or sit in the stand, asking themselves why they force themselves to suffer in this way. Yet every year, come June or July, they find themselves irresistibly drawn to the club offices, compulsively filling in their names on the season ticket application form, and condemning themselves to another nine months of purgatory. I'm convinced that home fans such as these see matches in quite a different way from myself and other fans who see most of their games away from the Racecourse. There is a difference between watching at home and watching away. When you watch a home match, you expect the team to win and play well. You'll support them and give them encouragement, of course, but there is a limit to your patience. At away games, you will put up with a lot more: you are on enemy territory. Your backs are up against the wall. Let's face it, most of the time, you'll settle for a point.

When I talk to friends who live in Wrexham and who watch the team week in, week out, I sometimes think we watch two different teams. Opinions of particular players vary so wildly that it's as if the player takes on a whole new identity when he travels to away games.

As examples, let's take two stalwarts of the current club line-up, Tony Humes and Steve Watkin.

Humes is a battling centre-back who, I think, has done well in recent memory in dealing with some heavy bombardments from opposing attacks. I think the partnership he's put together with Brian Carey is the main reason for the number of clean sheets we've kept since the big, ginger Irishman arrived at the club. If you watch Humes at home matches only, though, you see a different picture, and I can understand why some home fans have got a lower opinion of him. For them, he is a talentless clogger, unable to find his team-mates with a pass of anything more than two yards, and equally unable to time a tackle to coincide with the arrival of the ball rather than a defender's legs. I have to agree with them that he's never far away when there's a bit of fisticuffs, and his dire disciplinary record speaks for itself.

Steve Watkin– now at Swansea – has done well for us in most games that I've seen. He holds the ball up well and often taking a real pummelling from opposition defenders without resorting to the sort of whinging and lashing out tactics which have made Mark Hughes so widely despised by non-supporters of Man United, Chelsea and Wales. Home fans saw his inability to take on defenders and his poor goalscoring record and think he's a donkey. Swansea fans that I know are very disappointed with him.

Anyone who's travelled to an away game knows how it is that a woeful team performance – like the one I mentioned at Peterborough in 1989-90 – seems that much worse when it is followed by a long train or bus journey to allow extra time for reflection. And there have been some woeful, woeful days out for Wrexham fans in the last few years.

In the same way, of course, occasions where the team has done well can be savoured at greater length on a return journey. Our performances during this year's cup run have made for some of the most enjoyable away trips in recent years: Rooster's incredible last-minute winner at West Ham, the unprecedented performance at London Road and the tremendous victory at St Andrews. Another occasion which sticks in my memory is the night when we won promotion at Northampton in 1993 – the last significant post-match pitch invasion I remember. (A friend of mine still has a piece of County Ground turf

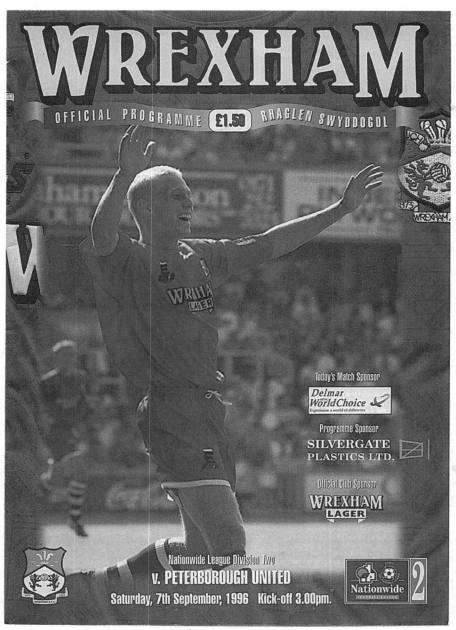

Wales' premier team?

in a jar on the mantelpiece!) This was the game Joey Jones put on a par with the night he won the European Cup with Liverpool in 1977 (Joey truly is our hero!). Anyway, after the game we made our way back to the station and waited in small groups for our train back down to London, only to be joined on the platform a few minutes later by none other than Jimmy Case, on loan to us from Brighton at the time. Ever the consummate professional (Brian Flynn once said that he was the best signing he'd ever made), he had evidently chosen not to take part in whatever post-match celebrations were going on in the dressing room. Instead he set out on his trip back down south with us, a classic example of the 'journeyman' footballer.

It goes without saying (although I'm afraid I'm going to say it anyway) that for a match to be really enjoyable we need to win: win comfortably, win with a last-minute goal, win with a last-minute shot from 35 yards, win luckily, win by the skin of our teeth, win by a total and unjustifiable fluke. At an away game, though, it is possible for us to be satisfied with less than a victory: in some circumstances, any result which represents a level of respectability will do.

A trip to an away ground is in every way a challenge. We take on the opposition players, of course, but also their manager, coaching staff and fans. In fact, sometimes the odds are so highly stacked against us that it feels like their whole town is against us. The one figure usually responsible for such a feeling taking hold is the referee. Correct me if I'm wrong, but isn't it his job to be an impartial observer, make each decision on its merits and **not** be swayed by the home crowd getting on his back, questioning his eyesight and his parentage (as home crowds have every right to)? How many times have the best efforts of Wrexham players faltered hopelessly when the red mist descends around the man in the middle and he suddenly points to the penalty spot or inexplicably reaches for a red card?

There is nothing to compare, in my view, with the sinking feeling in the pit of your stomach when a desperate struggle against the odds suddenly becomes totally hopeless. The moment when a power-crazed referee singles out an unsuspecting Wrexham player and, to the amazement of all concerned, sends him for an early bath. When events take such a turn and we lose anyway, the visiting supporters, myself included, are quite happy to clap the team off the pitch, satisfied that there was no way, in view of the odds stacked against us, that we were going to come away with even a draw. In fact, a 1-0 defeat really represents a moral victory on our part. Surely, in view of the circumstances, there should be an immediate intervention by the League Management Committee (or whatever they're called these days) to award us at least one point, and preferably all three.

So, how would I sum up the lot of the exiled fan? Looking back at the last few pages, I am struck by the number of times the words 'Peterborough' and 'woeful' appear, more often than not in very close proximity! So what am I saying? That I'd rather not be a Wrexham fan? But what else would I do instead? That I'd rather be a season ticket holder than have to watch most of my games away from home? Maybe.

One thing I do know, though, is that thanks to that fat Cockney geezer Barry Fry, Peterborough have been relegated to Division Three, and for me anyway, that's got to be a good result!

Chapter 11

Always the Bridesmaid
Mick Lehane

Of course, you realise we would have won the
World Cup by now if it wasn't for the bloody ref.

Watching Wales at international level could never be described as a boring experience -whatever else, you can guarantee that you will be subjected to a rollercoaster ride of emotions. Patronising commentators will always go on about the 'nearly men of world football' – 'always the bridesmaid' and other such infuriating comments.

The only time that Wales has managed to make it to the World Cup Final was in 1958, and even then they had lady luck to thank for their qualification. In their qualifying group they had finished runners-up to Czechoslovakia, but because of the political situation in Israel, no country in the Asian-African group some would play them. FIFA would not allow Israel entry to the World Cup without playing a game, so lots were drawn among the European runners-up and Wales was drawn out of the hat. Wales easily beat the Israelis home and away, and so qualified for the 1958 World Cup as the winners of the Asian-African group. Jimmy Murphy managed Wales at the time. As Wales were playing Israel in Cardiff on February 5th 1958, Murphy missed the ill-fated Manchester United trip to Belgrade where he should have been an assistant to Matt Busby.

Wales did well in the 1958 tournament – they drew all of their group games and were rewarded with a play-off game against Hungary to secure a quarter-final place. Wales won the play-off game 2-1 and so earned a quarter-final game against Brazil. However, time was against Wales on this occasion: the play-off game on June 17th was played in Stockholm and the quarter-final game was on June 18th in Gothenburg – a distance of 300 miles. Plus the great John Charles was missing for the game against Brazil. It is now history that Wales lost

1-0 to Brazil with some young upstart named Pelé scoring the winner. Whatever became of him, I wonder?

Welsh fans have now grown weary of hearing about 1958 – what was needed was some success for the current fans to savour. In the qualifying games for the 1978 World Cup in Argentina, Wales thought their chance had come. Because of a UEFA ban following crowd trouble in Cardiff, the match was played in Liverpool. It was felt that the Racecourse in Wrexham was too small. The plan backfired. Of the 51 000 crowd, most were Scots. The game will always be remembered for Joe Jordan showing Diego Maradona that 'the hand of God' originally belonged to him. Despite the cries of 'cheat' and protests from the Welsh, Don Masson scored the penalty and Wales were destined to spend the summer at home again.

Wales hoped that they would never see the Scots again, but the qualifying group for Mexico saw Wales again paired with Scotland, Spain and Iceland. As usual, Wales decided to make things difficult, losing the first two games away to Iceland and Spain. They eventually got the show on the road – beating Iceland 2-1 in Cardiff. When Ian Rush scored the only goal of the game at Hampden Park, the group was wide open. The win in Scotland went some way towards consoling the fans who still felt cheated by the Jordan handball incident in 1977.

Spain were next on the list and at the Racecourse in Wrexham, a crowd of 23 000 was not to be disappointed. Spain were overrun: two goals from Rush and a goal from Mark Hughes which has become a classic. The game, because of Hughes's goal, has become an 'I was there' occasion. Well, I was there, and since that night I think I have met about 150 000 other people who were there when Mark Hughes scored with his spectacular kick against Spain. For sheer quality, it has been matched only by Giggs's free-kick against Belgium.

The win against Spain meant that Wales would have it all to play for against the Scots in Cardiff. The winners of this game would earn the right to kick the crap out of Australia and qualify for the World Cup. After 14 minutes, Mark Hughes scored and Wales were on their way, but in the second half, the ghost of Joe Jordan returned to haunt Wales. A dreadful penalty decision against Dave Phillips meant the game was drawn and Scotland's superior goal difference gave them the runners-up spot. The disappointment of missing out was put into perspective when Jack Stein, the Scotland manager, suffered a fatal heart attack as the final whistle was blown.

The campaign for Italia '90 is best forgotten. Although it did see Wales draw 0-0 with West Germany at the National Stadium, soon after the Welsh FA decided to give up the nomadic trips around the country for international games and decided to play all games at the house of rugby in Cardiff.

The road to USA '94 could not have got off to a worst start: a 5-1 hammering away to Romania. Thankfully, I was spared having to witness this as on the night I was watching Barcelona against Samporia at Wembley. I watched the goal on the TV at Wembley and, to be honest, Wales were outclassed. So, another World Cup adventure was over before it started. Terry Yorath, the Wales manager, described the result as 'shocking' and must have welcomed the opportunity to put matters right 10 days later. Wales faced Holland in a friendly international in Utrecht. The team was under the temporary rule of Peter Shreeves because of the tragic death of Terry Yorath's son.

The game against Holland only highlighted the Welsh defensive problems. A 4-0 defeat was unlikely to restore confidence, following the result in Bucharest. The confidence in the Welsh camp must have been severely rocked by the two results. Before returning to the World Cup campaign, Wales flew to Japan to take part in the Kirin Cup – an international friendly competition involving Argentina and Japan. The opening game against Argentina did not produce the expected avalanche of goals, and over the 90 minutes Wales had the best chances. With two minutes remaining, Batistuta's free-kick beat Southall. Although Wales were beaten, the performances had been a big improvement on the previous two games. A meaningless game against Japan followed four days later and, to be honest, Wales made very hard work of their 1-0 win, although it could be argued that the controversial sending off of Iwan Roberts did not make the game easy for Wales. It was Wales's first victory in five games and it helped to get to get back to winning ways, which was the main thing following the results in Bucharest and Utrecht.

September 1992 meant a return to the serious business of World Cup qualification. Following the Romanian defeat, Wales's next opponents were World Cup minions, the Faroe Islands. The problem with such games is that you are in a no-win situation. Wales were expected to win and it was only the margin of victory that was in question. The final score of 6-0 was expected and it was a relief to see Wales restore some pride with a professional performance which ensured that the result was never in any danger.

The English tabloid press tried to make light of the result by making constant reference to Jens Martin Kaudsen's (the goalkeeper for the Faroe Islands) bobble hat! Little mention was made of the fact that they had beaten Australia and were technically very efficient. Granted they were the usual assortment of fork-lift truck drivers and bankers, but every year the FA Cup has such teams who can always manage one outstanding performance and Wales made sure that such a performance was not going to be at their expense.

This result was followed by a 1-0 win away in Cyprus. At this stage, the performance was not as important as the result; beating Cyprus meant that Wales kept on a winning run and also gained valuable points towards ultimate qualification. The next hurdle was going to be difficult and Wales failed the test. A 2-0 defeat by Belgium left Wales with a mountain to climb. Belgium and Romania were now in a commanding position in the group. There was a danger that the group would become a matter of pride if matters did not change. Following the defeat in Belgium, the next match for Wales was the return game in March 1993. The group table told its own story. Wales had to win to retain any hope of making it to the USA in 1994.

For many years, Wales led a nomadic existence when playing international football. The games alternated between Cardiff, Wrexham and, to a lesser extent, Swansea. Most of these 'home' games were dominated by club rivalries – away teams must have wondered what was happening when had an international match involved Welsh supporters sporting out club allegiances. It must have been very discouraging for the players because, in truth, the crowd never really supported them. The situation had deteriorated to such a level that programme notes would ask the supporters to get behind the national team and forget about club rivalries.

The decision to move to the National Stadium was an inspired choice; it had long been hoped that major internationals could be played there. The Welsh Rugby Union had also been against the idea of allowing football on their hallowed turf, although the ground is the oldest international venue in the world, with Wales playing some games there in the last century. The revolving ground situation had caused a north/south divide, and during Mike England's reign as manager, Wrexham was favoured. He felt the players felt more at home at the Racecourse. His rationale was that the major stars at the time, like Mark Hughes, Ian Rush, Neville Southall and Kevin Radcliffe, were all from North Wales and felt more at home playing there.

Whatever the politics behind this rotational ground scheme were, none of the grounds in question could claim to be international grounds. The argument would always end with Cardiff City claiming that Ninian Park could hold more supporters than the other options. This, of course, was true but in terms of facilities offered to the supporters, all grounds were equal – they were all sub-standard. The use of the National Stadium must have had a positive effect of the players. Even for fixtures against lesser opposition, like the Faroe Islands, the crowd felt a sense of excitement at the National Stadium. Players have described the ground as uplifting, and there was a feeling of passion and pride associated with representing your country at the National Stadium. Such feelings were never mentioned when playing at Ninian Park, the Racecourse or the Vetch. The move to the National Stadium also coincided with the disappearance of the moronic club chants which had dominated previous internationals. The sight of large crowds supporting Wales must have had a positive effect on the players.

In the run-up to the game with Belgium, much of the media speculation was on the performance of Ryan Giggs. He had arrived on the scene with some spectacular performances for Manchester United – he was already Wales's youngest international, making his debut at 17 years of age. The media were constantly harping on that the move to international standard was too much for such a young talent. International defenders would soon put him in his place. Terry Yorath did not allow Giggs to talk to the media, although one suspects this was on the instructions of Alex Ferguson.

The Belgium game would be Giggs's sixth international and he had yet to find the net. Well, 'cometh the hour, cometh the man'. Eighteen minutes into the game, we were awarded a free-kick. You could sense the anticipation as Giggs placed the ball. Very few players have this ability, to excite a crowd by their very presence. He is a rare and exceptional talent.

His free-kick will be remembered for ever by those fortunate enough to witness it. Even the Belgian supporters felt they had to applaud. Ian Rush scored a second before half-time. Belgium were always second best on the night and Wales proved that they had the players who could cope on the big stage and who would provide a result when it mattered most. The dream of America was alive again.

Wales faced two games away from home following the performance against Belgium. In April 1993 they travelled to Ostrava to meet the RCS, the representatives of the Czech and Slovakia Republics. Because this was the last competition in which they would take part as a combined team, it was always difficult to gauge their form. As the country was dividing, it was hoped that the players would look forward to international careers with their respective countries and that the combined team would just play out the fixtures. Wales could not have hoped for a better start when Mark Hughes opened the scoring after 29 minutes, but the joy was short-lived when Latal equalised nine minutes later. That was how the match finished. But Wales must have looked upon the result as points lost for they were much the more positive side and were denied by some resolute defending by the RCS.

The final away fixture was in Toftir, the Faroe Islands, on June 6th 1993. The usual media nonsense about the islanders abounded – the famous bobble hat was back and, of course, plenty of references to sheep. A major issue never given much mention was that this fixture came at the end of a very long season for the Welsh players. It was out of season really, and possibly not the best decision taken by the Welsh FA when they sat down to agree the fixture lists. Again, it was a no-win situation for Wales. Despite the fixture being out of season and being played on a different surface, Wales's Dean Saunders opened the scoring after 23 minutes with Young and Rush adding to the scoreline. A comfortable win was achieved and, in truth, Wales were never in any danger.

So, as this group closed down for the summer, Wales could be confident of progressing from the group. They now had nine points, a similar total to Romania and the RCS. But Wales had the comfort of their final three games in the group being at home, which meant that the RCS and Romania would have to travel to Cardiff and get a result for USA 1994. Perhaps the Welsh FA had got it right when the fixture list was discussed: home advantage for the final three games would be crucial.

September 8th 1993 – the RCS at the National Stadium. Wales started poorly and were very unsure. When Kuka scored after 16 minutes, there was a sinking feeling among the crowd, but if the crowd were beginning to feel frustration, the players certainly were not. The goal seemed to stir Wales into action and it was not long before Ryan Giggs had scored the equaliser. Wales continued to dominate and it was no surprise when Ian Rush put Wales in front after 35 minutes.

After half-time, Wales continued to dominate and should have put the result beyond question before disaster struck. A free-kick by Dubousky brought the RCS back into the game. You had to admire the skill of the goal but it was against the run of play and despite relentless pressure, Wales could not regain the lead. This was another game against the RCS that Wales must have looked upon as points lost. The group situation remained the same with any two from four capable of securing the all-important top two positions.

Belgium, the group leaders for so long, were beginning to falter, but for Wales the situation looked simple – win the remaining two games and qualification was guaranteed. The penultimate game of the group saw Cyprus visit the National Stadium on October 13th, 1993. This was without doubt the roughest match of the group. The Cypriots had obviously come to defend and keep the score down at any cost. Wales had to withstand some vicious tackling and provocation and also had to be patient in their approaching. Referee Philip Don had had enough of the nasty tactics and dismissed the Cypriot Costas Costa. The sending-off did not manage to quell the tempers of the Cypriots and it was obvious that retaliation for their kicking of the Welsh would be administered before the end of the game.

The patience of the Welsh paid dividends when Dean Saunders scored after 21 minutes. Ian Rush ensured that the points were safe with a second Welsh goal four minutes from the end. With the points safely secured, Wales should have been happy, but the continued physical nature of the game had a far from happy ending. Mark Hughes – who had been kicked from the very start of the game – had finally had enough. Hughes obviously felt that he was not being protected by the referee and decided to take matters into his own hands. His moment of madness earned him a booking, but much worse was to follow. The booking meant that he would be unavailable for the final match of the group against Romania. Players like Mark Hughes are irreplaceable – he is known as a man for the big occasions, as his countless goals in important games for Manchester United have proved. As usual, if Wales were to achieve the necessary results, it would have to be done the hard way.

November 17th 1993. The group table was the most complicated of all the World Cup groups:

Belgium – 14 points

Romania – 13 points

RCS – 12 points

Wales – 12 points

The simple solution was that Wales had to win to be sure of qualifying. The build-up to the game was unprecedented in Welsh football. Newspaper and TV coverage was at saturation point; in Wales, media scrutiny of this nature is usually reserved for rugby.

The first half was a very tense affair, but given what was at stake for both sides, you can understand why. Hagi opened the scoring for Romania after 32 minutes and you could sense the feeling among the crowd that this was going to be another night of heartache. However, if anything, the goal seemed to inspire Wales and they certainly had the better of the closing stages of the first half.

Wales started the second half with a passion not witnessed before and the reward arrived on the hour when Saunders equalised. Continuous Welsh pressure paid off with a penalty kick being awarded – qualification was now assured. Paul Bodin stepped up to take his place in Welsh football history. When his kick hit the cross bar, his place in history was assured, but for the wrong reason. The silence was deafening and a feeling of disbelief filled the ground. The Romanians, who had been reeling under the constant Welsh pressure, knew that they had been let off the hook. Wales searched in vain for the winner, and it was almost inevitable that the Romanians would clinch a goal, which duly arrived when Raduciou scored in the 82nd minute. When the final whistle blew, I saw grown men cry. Again, it was not to be for Wales.

Feelings of despair at the result were soon put in perspective with the news that an elderly man had died when he was hit by a distress flare at the match. If ever Bill Shankly's comment had a hollow ring, it was on this occasion – football is not more important than life.

Since that fateful night, the fortunes of Welsh football have been in reverse. The disgraceful treatment of Terry Yorath by the Welsh FA has left many supporters wondering if the powers that be in Welsh football really want success at international level or if they use their position to settle old scores. Yorath never appeared to be popular with the FAW and when the opportunity to get rid of him came, they took it. His contract was not renewed and John Toshack took over.

Toshack needed only one game, against Norway in March 1994, to realise all was not well with Welsh football. He claimed that he was not fully informed of the circumstances surrounding Yorath's removal. He resigned to leave Mike Smith to lead Wales for the Euro '96 qualification programme. The programme was a disaster with embarrassing defeats against Georgia home and away and Moldova away. Wales had become the whipping boys of the group. Smith did not see out the programme, being replaced by Barry Gould following the home defeat by Georgia. The appointment of Gould hardly inspired the supporters; there were other bigger names to choose from but they were ignored.

Wales suffered their heaviest defeat in over 60 years when they were trounced 7-1 in Holland. Another heavy defeat in Turkey has done little to restore confidence. In FIFA's world ranking, Wales are outside the top 100. It is painful to say, but Bobby Gould appears to be out of his depth at international level.

Wales has the players, like Giggs and Hartson, but the squad recently included a League of Wales players, suggesting that there is

1-0 up and then enter . . . Pierre Van Hooijdonk.
Final score: 3-1 to Holland,

any strength in depth with the system. How much longer will Wales have to wait to make their mark at international level? It is time to be at the top table of international football and time to forget the near misses, bad refereeing decisions and missed penalties. It must be time to achieve at international level. Being honest, the situation can hardly get any worse than it is now, and this without a real home to play in and Italy for good measure. Too daunting for even the most optimistic of Welshmen, surely?

Chapter 12

From the Table Top to Wembley Stadium

Dave Naylor

Subbuteo was an escape, then it became reality.

It all began for me in 1967, when I watched my dad fill in his pools coupon. As an inquisitive six-year-old who enjoyed kicking a ball around in the backyard, I wondered what all the fuss was about, putting crosses in boxes next to the various towns and cities in Britain. Of course, I knew that Swansea, Cardiff and Newport were the three teams that I recognised and wanted to win as they were Welsh. Swansea and Cardiff were also within travelling distance of home. Looking at the other teams on the coupon, Wrexham also stuck out – not because they were also Welsh (I wasn't totally aware that they were at that time!) – but because my grandparents' dog was called Rex! Looking further down the coupon, the Scottish divisions came into view. I'd heard of Celtic and Rangers, but didn't know where they came from, then I saw Montrose – yes I'll go for them (I used to love watching a series on TV called 'The Monroes', which sounded like Montrose so they had to be good!). Then I saw Hamilton Academicals! What's the connection as regards supporting them you may ask? Well, my dad worked in a chemical works, add a touch of rhyming slang 'chemicals – academicals' – yes, I'll go for them as well! So far I had spread my allegiance to teams covering the bottom half of the coupon and I hadn't picked any team from the top. There was a team called Man Utd – funny name I thought, why call a team Man, why not woman or boys? When I enquired further my mum said that was Bobby Charlton's team. Manchester United – all my mum's family in Gibraltar supported them (so she said), so I went for them as well! Apparently my first taste of watching football on the TV was a brief but noisy sojourn. We were on holiday in Gibraltar at the time of the 1966 World Cup, visiting my mum's family. It was the big one: England against West Germany. All the family were there watching intently and cheering England on, but I tried to ruin the occasion by shouting, running around and then crying so loudly that my mum had to cart me out of the house and take me for a walk to calm me down! A very long walk, presumably, due to a little thing called extra time – who said football was a game of two halves! Come 1968, and I was ready to receive my next dose of televised football. After playing a game of football down the field, it was a mad dash home to watch Man United take on Benfica in the European Cup Final. Sitting with mum, peering through what appeared to be a snowstorm but was just lots of interference on our old Ferranti television set, we saw a great game and Man United thrashing Eusebio and Co. Only another year to wait and I would see my first live match. That moment duly arrived on the 1st October 1969 (a Tuesday or Wednesday, I recall – certainly mid-week). A good friend of mine, Andrew, who lived down the hill in the next street, had been initiated into the world of live football much earlier as his dad used to take him to all the Cardiff home games. The invitation to come along was always there, but money was the big problem. Dad didn't earn too much and was not a football aficionado. He used to moan when my mum bought me *Goal* and *Football Monthly*, so to persuade him to let me go to a game was a major achievement in negotiation, manipulation and marketing skills, attributes which are now a dim and distant memory! I wasn't the only one being 'initiated', there were four of us and also Andrew and his cousin Chris. Life is a funny old thing. When you're really looking forward to something special, time goes so slowly and when the event arrives, time goes into warp factor speed – things never change, it's just the same now as it was back in October 1969. October 1st seemed to go so slow. Maths in the morning followed by 'Singing Together'. (Older readers may remember when you listened to a crackly old Radio programme called 'Singing Together' or 'Time and Tune' as part of Radio 4's school programmes. They'd play the song on the radio and you'd sing along to it from your song sheet. At the end of term you voted on your favourite song, a school kids' Eurovision Song Contest so to speak – still, I digress.) Then it was English in the afternoon. Finally, a quarter to four and..Oh joy! The bell, it's home time and only a few hours to go before my first live game – a European Cup Winners cup-tie between Cardiff City and the Norwegian Cup winners, Mjondalen.

Cardiff had already won the first leg away by 7 goals to 1, so the home leg was either going to be a formality or the mother of all European games. The walk home was a mile of constant anticipation and discussing with Andrew what the final score would be – the consensus of opinion was that if Cardiff could score 7 goals away from home, then it would be well into double figures at Ninian Park. After waving goodbye to Andrew for the moment, I ran up and over the hill and into the house. Mum was just cooking the tea – meatballs in tomato sauce and potatoes – funny how you remember the trivial things on special occasions! 'Wolfing' wasn't quite the word to describe how I ate, but if the late Roy Castle had been present in the kitchen, I would have been in the 1970 edition of the *Guiness Book of Records*! Out of the house and up and over the hill again to Andrew's house, but without a scarf (mum said that she would knit me one when she got some blue and white wool!). I got into his dad's Zephyr 6 and met all the other boys and away we went, down to Sandfields to pick up Chris. The adventure had begun, we were on the road!

We went through Pyle, Bridgend and Cowbridge, the highlight of the journey being the speedometer touching 100mph (strictly off the record of course, if any policemen, past or present, are reading this). After parking up we all shuffled along towards the ground and then to the Canton Stand (the seated area behind the goal). It cost 10 shillings (50p) to get in, as I remember. And there it was, the green turf shining under the floodlights – Utopia! As for the game itself, I don't remember much about it except that Mjondalen played in a mauve-coloured jersey with white shorts and they did score one to Cardiff's five. To cap a great evening, another young lad who sat near us had a rattle and he let me have a go – the night's initiation complete! I attended a few more games at Ninian Park, but it's true what they say – as you get older, you get wiser. As I got older I realised that I was really a Jack at heart – the ace of clubs for me was Swansea City. The Vetch would have to wait a few years. Meanwhile, it was more football down the field and in the living room with my brother, using 2 fireguards as goals and a crumpled newspaper as a ball! Summer evenings were spent on the grassed areas bordering Aberavon Beach as 12 of us (yes,

12!) travelled down in the Zephyr 6 to have a kick about. I've had some embarrassing moments in goal for the Gloucester Swans in recent years but none worse than in one of those beach games back in the early 1970s.

Halfway through a great game, a dog appeared and joined in – not on any one side, just trying to get the ball off whoever had it. This dog was one hell of a player though, using only its nose it was the George Best of the canine community of Aberavon, so we called it Pelé, Pelé the dog! Not only did it have good ball control on the ground, it also, as I found out to my utter amazement, had the quality of a Ron or Wyn Davies in the air! The other side attacked down our left flank and an inch-perfect (metrication was only just coming in at the time) cross was put into our goalmouth. But to who? From nowhere, Pelé the dog ran in unmarked, leapt up and let loose with a bullet-like header past yours truly! Unfortunately, the ground beneath me didn't open up and I was forced to trudge behind the goal, with the ecstatic dog bounding ahead, to retrieve the ball. The ritual humiliation of my goalkeeping skills lasted for several weeks. Every dog has its day, that was Pelé's – we never saw him again. I did redeem some pride in a game between class 3A Cwmavon Juniors against Standard 3 played in the Pant, a Wembley Stadium without the seats, a natural amphitheatre of a place near the River Afan. You could even have a half-time drink from a spring nearby, although it was always a scramble to get there first just in case one of the opposition pissed in the water!

Anyway, back to the game, where I was playing in midfield. The opposing team's keeper kicks out and, standing just inside my own half, I volley the ball back to where it came from, but this time past the keeper and into what would have been the back of the net. In reality there were just two sticks and a lot of fresh air, but a goal to remember, nevertheless. Meanwhile, indoors, the fireguards had been replaced by the new, realistic game of football called Subbuteo. This was real hands-on stuff – no computer games and Jim Rosenthal commentaries then! You made your own commentaries and your own football leagues, resulting in quite absurd finales. For example, in my league Aldershot won the championship! I started playing Subbuteo on the floor. Firstly on lino, which was a dead loss because the ball used to skid off the surface so quickly and so far that I spent more time retrieving it from the hallway than playing a game! Then we had a carpet laid down – unfortunately it wasn't one of those level carpets but one with 'dimples' in, so the game took ages to complete. There were also quite a few injuries to the players, due to my brother, sister or mother stepping on them! Out with the Airfix glue – by the end of a game I was as high as Aldershot in my league (perhaps that's why Aldershot won my league!) Who needs glue bags when you've got injured Subbuteo players!

It all got a bit too much, people walking all over my pitch – it was then that my game graduated to the table top. There was still the odd injury as players tottered on the edge and then fell three feet on to the floor below – another injury, some more glue and a big smile on my face! The table-top stadium came of age as I made my own stands from the boxes of the other teams I had and used the teams themselves as spectators, except the goalkeepers, of course – trying to fit them in, rods and all, was impossible. Then one Christmas Santa brought me a proper Subbuteo pitch!The seventies had dawned, and my first Swans game! Whatever anyone says about the seventies, no one can deny that it was a decade full of variety and extremes, not only of fashion stereotypes and music but most other things you could think of. The football terraces saw all these various cult changes: from the skinhead/smoothies era, through the long-haired/scruff-cut/flared trousers phase of the mid 1970s to the punk/skinhead/mod phase at the end of the decade.1971-72 was well and truly in the skinhead/smoothie era. This was the time when your best mates were Ben Sherman and Doctor Martin (preferably the cherry red variety with about 30 lace holes that took about half a day to put on).

Other accessories for the trendy/hard football fan of this era were a pair of braces (even if you did have a belt on your trousers), a tank top, red socks, Arrington jacket, Levi Sta-Press and, for the smoothie or smartly dressed type, a Crombie and a pair of brogues. What's all this crap got to do with my first Swans game you way ask? Well, I'm just setting the scene, and, for those nostalgic gits like myself, taking a sentimental trip down memory lane. That season saw the Swans in the old Division 3, drawing crowds of 6000 or so, and also saw my first visit to the Vetch. Back in those days, the school playground at dinner time, when not transformed into mini-Wembley Stadia, became the spawning ground for that scourge of the 1970s – football hooliganism. Gangs of boys with allegiances to Swansea (always in the majority) and Cardiff (always in the minority) chased each other and did battle. Once the bell sounded to return to lessons, all was forgotten and everyone was the best of friends. In my class at school there was a lad called Stuart who was one of the hardest in the class. He was an ardent Swans fan who used to brag about some of the dubious characters he knew who followed the Swans, like, for example, a bloke called 'Big Dare', who often got into punch-ups with rival fans.

We were all gullible, easily-impressed 11-year-olds then, and when Stuart used to spin these yarns about the exploits of 'Big Dare' and others, like chasing Rhyl fans around the town before an FA Cup match, we were spellbound. It wasn't long, however, before the day came when I could impress Stuart. I used to nag my dad for ages to take me to a game but, not liking football, he would have none of it. He must have got a bit fed up though because one day he came home from work and said that Gareth, the son of some friends of my parents, was willing to take me to see the Swans play their next home game, which was against Bradford City. I couldn't wait – Bradford had one of the best strips in the League – yellow and red stripes with black shorts. I asked if Stuart could come along and it was okay. On a bright, October Saturday lunchtime, Stuart and I took the bus down to Port Talbot, walked to the railway station and met Gareth. He was kitted out in a Ben Sherman shirt, Arrington jacket, Levi Sta-Press, red socks, brogues and a black and white scarf, which he let me wear – Stuart was suitably impressed! Talking on the train and walking through Swansea, it turned out that Gareth was one of the 'in crowd' on the North Bank. I well remember us turning the corner down a street near the Vetch to see a gang of about 20 skins coming towards us. My heart almost stopped, but soon restarted when Gareth acknowledged them.

We all walked towards the North Bank and Gareth enquired at the turnstile as to which entrance boys of our age should go into. We were directed further along the North Bank and eventually ended up under the old Double Decker stand (now the west terrace). Before going in, one of the skinheads (called Brontus) tried to climb up a drainpipe to get over the top of the turnstile without paying, but was hauled down by a passing policeman before he was halfway up! That afternoon the 'North Bank Boys' were all under the Double Decker, cheering the

Swans on with songs such as the Swansea version of 'Cockles and Mussels' and Lee Marvin's 'Wandering Star'. For so long Stuart had impressed me with his tales, now I impressed him (and myself!) with the real thing as we stood among the chanting throng of the North Bank boys. To cap it all, the Swans won 2-0, including a penalty right in front of us! The Swans finished in a creditable mid-table position that season. Over the Christmas period they drew a crowd of over 20 000 when at home to the eventual champions, Aston Villa, who won the game 3-1. Thereafter, my live games were a bit thin on the ground until age and pocket money increased. Oh, and a certain John Toshack arrived at the Vetch. From that point on, Saturdays and Tuesdays would never be the same. Meanwhile, with my fellow supporter, Mr Armchair, the years slipped away before Tosh's arrival. In that time I played my one and only seriously competitive game of football for..Cwmavon Boys' Club! After nearly a whole season loyally attending training sessions, I was finally given my chance in the number 7 shirt at home to Nottage, who apparently weren't one of the better sides around. At half-time it was 1-1, still the same score when I was substituted 15 minutes from time. The final score – a 4-1 victory! Read into that what you will but I never played again – I didn't like the half-time oranges anyway! From then on it was the informal stuff, like our many arranged games against the boys from Bryn. Fond memories abound of piling on to a Llynfi bus and hoping to hell we didn't have to get out halfway up the hill to push the damn thing and then getting out in one piece at the other end as those automatic doors did a good impersonation of Jaws. I speak from experience after nearly being beheaded once as I struggled to get on the last bus out of Maesteg after an under-age night out viewing an X-cert movie at the Regal. Still I digress.

Bryn, as the name suggests, is a small village built on a hill. The football field is even higher up but did have 'real' goalposts. It was rumoured that the England 1970 World Cup squad cut their hit single 'Back Home' on the Bryn football field (they later mimed it on 'Top Of The Pops') as a form of altitude training in readiness for their group games at Guadalajara in the 1970 Mexico World Cup! Apart from vertigo and breathlessness, I usually ended up coming home mottled brown and smelling of sheep shit, and cut and bruised to buggery by the bulrushes which dotted the goalmouth – such is the life of a goalkeeper! One game that sticks out in my mind was a freezing cold Saturday morning affair when only six of us turned up. After conceding two goals in as many minutes, the referee took pity on us and played a dual role – still officiating, but also bolstering up our midfield. I conceded a further 14 goals that morning and our only chance of scaring a consolation came when Peter, our lone centre forward, struck the cross bar with an open goal below! The flight of the Swans up the divisions was a wonderful experience, goals galore and top-notch entertainment. My first ever away game was the long trek to Gillingham back in the autumn of 1973. The crowd of just over 11 000 was their highest for a long time. I remember meekly standing outside the turnstile with several others when, coming down the road towards us, we saw what appeared to be five men in white coats – a premonition of the future you may think after reading all this crap, but no! On closer inspection they were five skinheads in butcher's overalls (the word 'meatheads' came to mind but not to mouth). They paused to look us up and down and said, 'One, two, three..ten Swansea fans, take them easy.' But that was the last we saw of them. The game was a 2-0 defeat, but on the journey back the (then) famous Professor Magnus Pyke was spotted in the car park at Heston services. On the subject of celebrities, I saw Enoch Powell in a West London pub and have sat on the same seat as Jeremy Thorpe, but that's another story!

The 1978-79 season seemed to pass by so quickly, ending with the dramatic 2-1 win over Chesterfield at the Vetch. My lasting memory that night – apart from the long queues to get in – was the smell of aftershave! Nearly everyone around us seemed dressed up and ready to go out clubbing and celebrating after the game. Instead of coming home smelling of cigar smoke, lager or a urine- stained trouser leg, the aroma of Aramis and the presence of Paco Rabanne clung tightly to my bum-fluffed skin. The season of 1979-80 was one of consolidating a place in the 2nd Division before pushing for ultimate glory. Although starting work in the summer, I still managed to see most of the home games and many of the away games. The highlights of that season for me were the FA Cup games against Crystal Palace. After two breathtaking draws, the second replay was, after the toss of a coin, to be held at Ninian Park on a Tuesday – or was it Wednesday – night in January. Living in Barry at the time meant a short train trip but I managed to persuade one of my fellow lodgers, Steve (a fanatical Bolton

fan) to come along, so he drove. Due to the cold showers, we decided
to stand undercover on the Bob Bank – one of the three and a half
Swansea 'ends' that night. Ten minutes to kick-off and the atmosphere was building up nicely and, with the arrival of a few hundred
Cardiff fans in the Bob Bank, things kicked off before the game
started. Scenes of kids as young as ten and blokes in their forties
throwing punches and kicks at each other continued for about half an
hour into the game. There must have been a group of about 50 of us
forming an island of calm in the sea of mayhem going on all around
us. My mate Steve couldn't figure out why there should be Cardiff
fans there at all, let alone them shouting for the Eagles. Then an old
bloke standing next to him turned around and said, 'That's how dull
we Welsh are.' Never a more apt comment spoken in a moment of crisis. The police and their dogs appeared and some semblance of order
was restored. The attendance that night must have dropped by a
thousand or so towards the end of the first half as the police set to
work thinning out the crowd. It was easy to spot who was who: Swans
fans wearing black and white and Cardiff fans wearing donkey jack-
ets bearing the insignia NCB or CEGB and fluorescent orange or green
patches. Finally, one for the trivia buffs: the 25 000 there that night
was Ninian Park's highest League and Cup gate of the season, what
was the 'home' team? Answer - Swansea City!1980-81 was **the** promotion season, but as work increased my attendance at games
thinned out, although the 4-1 away victory at Burnden Park, while
standing in the Bolton end, was my highlight of the year (I missed the
Preston one), with a boozy weekend at Steve's to boot.

My season ticket for the Division 1 season was the best loan item
my brother ever had. For him, Christmas came every other weekend,
while for me it was frustration, *The Western Mail* and Radio Wales.
Then followed the decline and fall years, the downs and ups and then
1993-94 – Wembley! Before that, my seat in the grandstand amidst
the chaos at Ninian Park on a cold December evening marked a per-
sonal landmark – that of having watched a game from all four sides of
the ground at Ninian Park – not bad for a Swansea fan!

Ah, Wembley. Okay, so it was only the Autoglass Trophy final but
still, seeing one's club at Wembley is something you only dream
about. It makes up for all those dire games you've seen in the cold and
rain, and also for being called northern bastards by some kids in Ley-

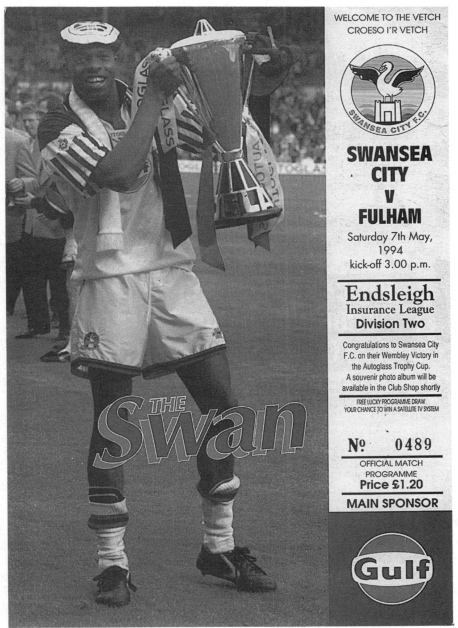

WELCOME TO THE VETCH
CROESO I'R VETCH

**SWANSEA
CITY
V
FULHAM**

Saturday 7th May,
1994
kick-off 3.00 p.m.

Endsleigh
Insurance League
Division Two

Congratulations to Swansea City
F.C. on their Wembley Victory in
the Autoglass Trophy Cup.
A souvenir photo album will be
available in the Club Shop shortly

FREE LUCKY PROGRAMME DRAW
YOUR CHANCE TO WIN A SATELLITE TV SYSTEM

№ 0489

OFFICIAL MATCH
PROGRAMME
Price £1.20

MAIN SPONSOR

Gulf

Cardiff City 1927 . . . Swansea City 1994. And that sir, is all you are getting.

tonstone before the Autoglass quarter-final game at Orient (they obviously took woodwork instead of geography at school). After a champagne breakfast, a mugshot in *90 Minutes* and a penalty win in extra time, the sight of that well-known Jack, Michael Howard, presenting the trophy to 'Super' John Cornforth nearly brought a tear to this delirious individual's eye. After building a Wembley Stadium out of Subbuteo team boxes, I had sat in the real thing, watching my team win a trophy. From the table top stadium to Wembley Stadium – a paradise lost and then regained.

Chapter 13

Flowers in the Dustbin
Sean Lewis and Keith Haynes

The big two from South Wales get an early wake-up call. Millwall reckon no one likes 'em, these two have no friends at all.

If one goes, we all go.

No matter who you follow in Wales, and I mean whether you are blue or white, the future for all supporters of Welsh club sides is looking bleaker by the week. Both Swansea City and Cardiff City now find themselves in the bottom half of the Third Division, unable to pull 5000 fans between them for home games, and financially in the hands of people who will not be around in five years' time if the situation does not improve. For years now we, as football supporters in the principality, have had the threat of expulsion to the League of Wales hanging over us. Many have debated the topic, few have really faced up to the fact that the current climate will almost certainly spell the end for the country's biggest football clubs.

Cardiff City

For any football fan, the prospect of a visit to Ninean Park leaves you wondering if you will go home to the family afterwards with all your body parts intact. This, as we know, is a falsehood, stories of hostile receptions from the locals are often exaggerated or untrue, the lunatic fringe only appears for the bigger games and they are few and far between these days. In recent times, only visits by Swansea City, Manchester City, Luton and maybe the odd team doing well have prompted the idiots to appear in any great number. And what of this particular individual? Ask any of them to name more than a couple of

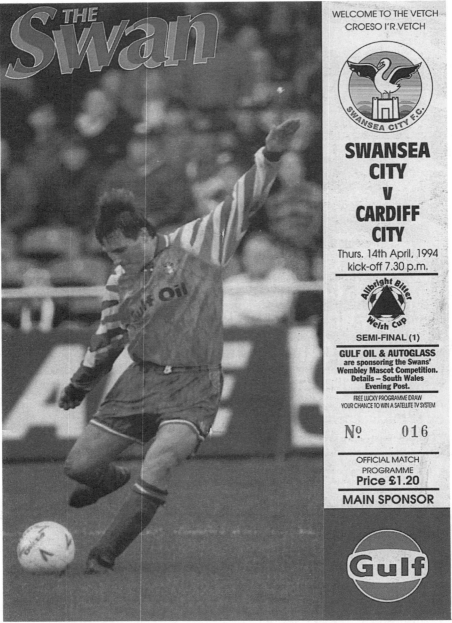

A much-talked about swimming competition in Mumbles Bay followed one Swansea v Cardiff clash, much to the amusement of all – well, Swans fans, anyway.

the side and they would struggle, so would they really care if their home town club went sliding down the pan? Probably not. Those who have visited Ninean in recent years to watch their side play and been on the receiving end of this sort of behaviour would more than likely breathe a huge sigh of relief if Cardiff went down to the League of Wales. And let's face it, even those who have never been there, preferring to hear the stories from friends who have braved the journey, would also cheerfully wave the Bluebirds goodbye. Why would this be? Well, for a start Cardiff City are Welsh, yes, sheep-shaggers of the first order, with stupid accents and fearful reputations throughout Europe. To the English football supporter they would be no real loss to the Football League, and to replace them with the likes of Stevenage or Cheltenham would be far more interesting. These days you look after your own and Wales ain't no way anything to do with England.

The Welsh have an aggressive hatred of all things English, much the same as the Scottish people have had for hundreds of years, however, that's where the similarity ends. This, however, pisses the English off in some style and understandably so. They often find themselves the main stay of the Union in the UK, facing the Welsh and Irish republican voices with their own form of nationalism. The stereotypical English lad has learned in recent times to fight back. They would love to see the Bluebirds further down the football ladder, or preferably not on it at all.

Let me give you a scenario. Cardiff City are facing expulsion from the Football League via the evil UEFA fools or financial ruin. Much the same as Brighton did, they appeal to all genuine football fans to rally round and show unity against the powers that be. What response would they get? Imagine the football fan who has braved the Cardiff trip to watch their team play responding positively to this appeal. If you can imagine that, you have the positive energy of a frantic poltergeist – no way would the Bluebirds ever get the support of the football fans of England. All the past would rear its ugly head, and to be quite frank the press outside Wales wouldn't give a toss either, they would also work to the same ethic. It would be left to the football fan in Wales to fight the corner and this is the whole point of the argument. UEFA would say, 'Well, the English don't want them in their league so its bye bye Bluebirds, who gives a toss if their own supporters care.' UEFA would pull the plug, no problem. The fact that until the early 70s Cardiff City was Wales's premier club would count for nothing. The FA Cup win of 1927 annoys even the most placid of Englishmen, all Cardiff City would become would be another pub quiz question. Nice epitaph.

Cardiff City could easily pull crowds of 40 000 plus in the fifties and sixties, even in the seventies they had their proud moments. Nowadays they have a hard-core of supporters, maybe 5000 on a good day, who really care about the club. This was summed up at a 1996 midweek Auto Windscreen Shield game at home, who turned up..just over 800, the lowest ever turnout that season in any competition. In fact, that night Kidderminster and Yeovil, two non-league clubs, had bigger gates for their own Mickey Mouse Trophy games. That comparison on its own is frightening. Even the most passionate Cardiff fans could draw little from this statistic, the same night the Swans pulled over 5000 for their equivalent tie against Bristol City, with only 200 visiting supporters. And this is my final point on the club, the Cardiff fans will always compare themselves to their fierce rivals from West Wales, whatever the point, be it attendances, transfers, Cup competitions, League position or recent fixtures. On most subjects in recent times the Cardiff fan has to bite the bullet here. Attendances at the Vetch over the past 20 years knock Cardiff's well into second place, even over the past few seasons the Swans have come out on top.

On transfers, the Swans have made millions; Cardiff nowhere near them again. Swansea City have made play-off finals and semi-finals, and won the Autoglass Trophy at Wembley. Results are even as you would expect, however, we return to my original point, who would support the Bluebirds if the chips were really down? Even in Wales it would be hard to find the backing from outside the club. Recent rivalries and clashes with the Swans put their supporters well out of the running, Wrexham are too far away and the League of Wales holds the only clubs who may support Cardiff, albeit to say they don't want them. The real Cardiff fan is the only one who suffers of course, as they always have. Some would say it was of their own doing, others would just smile. The plain fact is that if the Bluebirds fall, then this next lot would not be far behind.

Swansea City

For many years the Swans were the poor relations of Welsh football, never equalling their counterparts from Cardiff City on any scale, that is until Cardiff's own John Toshack took over at the club in the late seventies. Now I don't intend this to be a history lesson, Swansea's brief flirtation with Liverpool and Man United has been well documented many times before, but no mention of the club can go without this part of the club's history getting a mention. The Swans pulled in massive crowds during the 1981-82 season, 24 000 for the first game with Leeds United. Remember that 5-1 win? They were the country's heroes, outside of Cardiff that is. Liverpool, Man United, Arsenal and Man City all lost to Tosh's team that season, with attendances often in excess of 20 000. Those days are gone, but what days they were for the Swans fans. They finished sixth that season and with four games to go could and should have won what is now the Premiership title. Dark shadows are all that remain, and, of course, those awful, Danny Baker-type memory lane programmes.

In recent times the Swans have kept their heads above water by selling many of their better players. Take a good look around the upper tiers of the Football League and you will see millions of pounds' worth of talent plying their skills in the Premiership and First Divisions. Even today, the Swans are looked upon as a good place to shop for young talent. City, itself, claims to be the heart of sport. However, this is debatable. Current owners Silver Shield have felt a massive backlash to poor results, much the same as Mr Kumar down the road. Real football fans vote with their feet, and when something's not right they do so in their thousands. There are many similarities to Cardiff City here, and no matter what the individual supporters of both clubs think, they are well and truly staring non-league football in the face. Both clubs are now relying on success and success of the financial sort has never been easy to get when you are in the lower parts of the League. FA Cup runs and one-off appearances at Wembley may sustain the club for a few weeks but Swansea, according to their owners, are leaking money quicker than the Titanic engine room leaked water and the future is hardly stable. Swansea could easily be the first to leave the Football League. The company running the club is very much linked to the City and the fragile futures that today's economy brings. This in some ways is tragic, after all since 1912 the people of Swansea have enjoyed first-class football, why should the greed and influence of London decide the future of the club?

Unfortunately, football has let itself fall into the economic trap of the City – the lust for wealth and success of the likes of Manchester United is hard to ignore, especially when you are facing extinction at every turn. Premiership football and TV also has the blame lying firmly at their door, and what of the Football League itself? They too have many questions to answer. Success can only be shared by the few whilst the likes of Swansea City scramble for the crumbs that are left behind. Much the same as Cardiff, they hope and pray for big ties and TV money to keep going. The majority of Third Division clubs have the threat of closure hanging over them, Welsh clubs, as I have said, have the added threat of UEFA and the League of Wales to contend with.

African nations are now demanding a bigger and louder say in the world game and this filters its way down to the Vetch field in a strange way. The Africans rightly point to the four football associations of the UK, all with votes and agendas that outweigh the many countries that are Africa. The UK is smaller, has little or no success and yet still has a very loud shout in world football matters. With the attention on the UK, increasingly questions are being asked. We are British when it suits; and individuals also to our own liking. UEFA have already forced the three professional football clubs of Wales in the English Football League to stop participating in the Welsh Cup for the right to play in Europe. How much longer will it be before they go the whole way? Swansea City are so small on the English stage, let alone the European one, that they would crumble quickly if pressure was brought to bear on them, much the same as Cardiff. They would find no support from the English clubs and fans. Swansea's own supporters hardly wear haloes, and have been caught up in awful crowd scenes in recent years followed by fines and threats of closure. To put it mildly, Swansea and Cardiff have resembled leper colonies during the nineties. No one likes them, and to be honest they do care.

Outside of football, Swansea has found itself in the spotlight recently with the film *Twin Town* being touted around the UK's cinemas in 1997, and Welsh bands finding themselves with plenty of publicity throughout the year. Have you noticed that no one ever asks the Manics who they support? I recall as a young punk rocker in the late seventies, wishing for the success enjoyed by today's Welsh bands. It almost became trendy this year to be Welsh – bloody frightening! Who wants the Americans claiming Welsh ancestry as they do with the Irish? Having said that, I would love to introduce the Yanks to some of our much-revered pastimes, should get rid of them pretty quickly. What I do find amusing about Swansea is that the links the city has with current stars, even the links Wales has, are very quickly broken. Kevin Allen, the writer and maker of *Twin Town*, mentions his roots in the city, but these days he wouldn't be seen dead on the North Bank. David Baddiel would tell you a similar tale, but how many of you know that Suggsy from Madness wrote 'Baggy Trousers' about Haverfordwest Grammar School? Hardly the good old London lad really, well until the PR men got hold of him, just not trendy you see. Eddie Izzard speaks affectionately about being brought up in Wales, yet all of these folk have something in common: they couldn't give a fuck about the country really, and who can blame them?

This is the root of the Swans' problems, all those who could do something for the club don't, and those that do could easily make an overnight escape back to the sprawling metropolis of London, that is if the stock market made it financially cheaper to do a runner than stay and keep the club afloat at a loss. And why should we blame them? You get little thanks in the game of football for wearing your heart on your sleeve. Silver Shield have found this out at Swansea, all they will get is a constant stream of abuse if they stay and even worse if they go. Doug Sharpe, the previous owner, found this out at an early stage of his ownership of the club. Following your team is a hobby, apparently a release from the pressures of everyday life. Would you, if you had the money, buy your club and put up with the shite these people have to endure? Think about it. Currently, Silver Shield hold the future of the club in their hands, if it goes wrong they would make good their escape as any business would. Going wrong in this case is a failure to win promotion next season, being quietly booted out of the Football League is not on their agenda, however it is a possibility they would be foolish to ignore.

Looking Ahead

If this were an end of term report, both Swansea and Cardiff would be facing the bleak prospect of the jobcentre and many years on the dole. 'Could do better,' would be an often-used phrase. With football racing away with odd ideas, and mad chairmen with only their own agendas and profiles to maintain, the Swans and Bluebirds are desperately hanging on to their futures by their fingertips. The supporters are worried about just what or who will be playing in their colours from month to month and if any of these individuals really care. This plight is not unusual throughout the world, however, the future of a country's sport is at stake here. With respect, it's not as if Hereford's or Doncaster's plights are anywhere near as important, or even Brighton's for that matter. None of us would really care if they went AWOL tomorrow, they hardly represent their country's future, but Swansea and Cardiff do. And again, with all due respects to Wrexham, if one of these two went then the rest would almost certainly follow, and then who would everyone hate, sheep and all?

Chapter 14

Final Thoughts
Keith Haynes

The harsh reality of it all – but it's only a game really!

I set out in the spring of 1997 to write a book about football, to contribute to the world's biggest game in some way, to have my small say on the things that really matter to us football fans. I didn't think it would be about Welsh football, that bit just happened. As I have said, I didn't want to include the darker side of the game. We, as Welsh football fans, have seen too much of this element in recent times. However, I had to. That is a fact of life, something we all have to recognise and address. I consider myself fortunate that I have managed to complete the book in a reasonably short period of time: it is now March 1998.

Welsh football is either in a long transition period or reaching the end of the road, I just hope the former is the path we are taking. The alternatives, which are well documented here, do not bear thinking about. When you look back to the past and former glories of our football clubs, you realise that none of us has ever really set the world alight, but that is not the point. There have been better times and those times can return with the correct structure and people running our football clubs. The Swansea City team of the early eighties was a fine side built on confidence and passion, their colleagues from the fifties were a better side in a harder, more realistic world. Wrexham's exploits in the FA Cup are commendable, especially the side which reached the quarter-finals during the 1996-97 season. To see them beat West Ham at Upton Park was a pleasure, the reaction from the home supporters was even more surprising. They applauded the Wrexham team and supporters after running onto the pitch. This shows just how far football fans have come in the past ten years. This would never have happened during the days of the infamous West

Ham 'chicken run'. We have come a long way, but there is still much to do.

Cardiff City is the name on everyone's lips in Wales when success is discussed. They are sleeping giants, but when will they wake up? When will they realise the ambition of their supporters? Very few Cardiff City supporters can remember the heady days that involved their team during the fifties and sixties, only a handful recall that famous day in 1927 when they won the FA Cup. We all cling on to one-off memories, not whole seasons of glory, not whole decades like Liverpool and Manchester United fans can. They have been spoilt, but at least they realise that teams like the Welsh three are the future of the game. Newport County's demise as a Football League club must have been harrowing for their supporters, it is unlikely that they will ever return to the Football League, although it is clearly their ambition to do so. They have done remarkably well to get to their current position and there is no doubt that they could sustain a Football League club in Gwent, especially now that football has an even wider audience through the medium of television.

The smaller landmarks in the Welsh game have slowly eaten away at the heart of Welsh football. The decision to remove Cardiff City and Swansea City from the Combination League for reserve teams for the 1997-98 season was a massive blow. The London clubs voted them out of the league, stating it was too far to travel. Both clubs now scratch around looking for a game, hardly conducive to bringing on the talent of the future. And what of that talent? The Swans have a superb record of selling on players to bigger clubs, the list is endless. They have made a fortune from the transfer fees of these individuals, just to prop up the club. Cardiff City have always failed to achieve in this department and have a host of 'nearly' players who should have gone on to bigger and better clubs. So how have they survived?

The fact that they have is a credit to the club's administration, surprised? Their dilapidated Ninean Park ground is ripe for development, just waiting for the right person to step in and give them the facilities they need to be a good First Division or even Premiership club. But, of course, you can't do this without the players, and this is where the Welsh FA should be involved. Okay, they have commendable football schools and have many working at the grass roots of the game to bring on these youngsters, but more can be done, much more.

It has long been believed that rugby is the dominant force in Wales and takes the cream from the top of the gifted pile of Welsh sportsmen and women. The Welsh FA is a faceless body of elected men who the fans do not identify with. Very few of them are known to the real fans on the terraces. Do they really have their fingers on the pulse of the national game? Because football is the national game, even in Wales. It is well documented that more people are actively involved in football than rugby at the grass-roots level. More people play football than rugby in this small country of ours. The league systems throughout the country are massive and are an untapped source of talent, so why do they play on Saturdays, forcing the active football fan to choose between playing and watching football? The attendances would increase tenfold if Wales had a successful football club to watch on a Saturday afternoon. During the rise of Swansea City, the Saturday Swansea League was moved and at times cancelled to accommodate the urge to watch instead of play. This should be the norm, not the exception. Welsh rugby itself is in a long transition phase, the switch to the professional game has been hard to take for some and the attempts to copy the success of football have been amateurish and ill considered. They will pay a hefty price in the years to come.

The faceless few at the Welsh FA have much to learn and even more to contribute to turn our game around. Alun Evans once fronted the Welsh FA and he paid for his high profile, he became a hated figure, the brunt of the anger and frustration. He blustered his way through his appointment, finding himself in the spotlight during the inception of the League of Wales. He spent unnecessary time in court with the teams who refused to join the new league and earned himself many enemies. However, Alun Evans, much the same as Gordon Taylor, will tell you he is a football fan, someone who has the future of the game at heart, but to what ends? His downfall came with the negotiations of Terry Yorath's new contract as Welsh manager. He looked a relieved man when he left his post. Many cheered, but the reality of the situation was that Terry Yorath was replaced and the national team has been on a slippery slope ever since. The boat was again missed. Alun Evans still has an active role at the Welsh FA but these days he takes a more subtle and silent approach, he has learned the hard way.

The Welsh press gives considerable coverage to the game, and they too have much to answer for. The lust for success has clouded their judgement and many football fans will tell you of the bias towards Cardiff City from the newspapers and media. The fans have had enough. Radio programmes featuring views of supporters rarely have input from Swansea and Wrexham fans because they have long given up on the hope that an equal time will be had by all. The BBC is known in South Wales as 'The Bluebird Broadcasting Corporation'. The reasons why are obvious and simple: the BBC is based in Cardiff and there is a dominance of Cardiff folk at the company. It goes without saying that they will dwell on the fortunes of Cardiff City. What they fail to realise is that the national papers and media should be just that, they are not a local thing and never have been. I have noticed a small change of heart in the past year or two, but it is very small, again there is much to do.

So what positives can we draw upon for the future? Swansea City have plans in place for a new all-seater ground for 25 000 to be based at The Morfa site on the outskirts of Swansea, and aim to make it to Division One in five years. This is slightly laughable since they stated in 1997 that the plan would take them to the Premiership. The owners of the club have had a sticky ride from the fans since 1997 and rightly so. They will not be bluffed by the PR that comes with club take-overs and commercial ventures. It seems that the owners of this particular club have been given time to prove themselves to the fans. I personally wish them well in their plans and their vision, again what's the alternative? At the moment, it's John Hollins and a tale of what might be.

Cardiff City are currently owned by a Birmingham businessman, he too has visions for the future and longs for success. Since he bought the club, Cardiff City have stuttered and failed to achieve. There seems very little to make the fans optimistic. Mr Kumar must sometimes wonder just what he has got himself into, a recent deal with the ice hockey club promised the much-needed cash required to get them out of the Third Division. The money was spent and Cardiff City looked like a team that just might do something, on paper they looked strong. Unfortunately, the paper talk failed to transmit itself to the field of play and Cardiff are still in the Third Division, still hoping. Frank Burrows has returned to Cardiff for the 1998/99 season – the offer to "never return" will soon be tested.

Wrexham, much the same as Swansea, finance their immediate future with the sale of players. Again it makes you wonder just where they would be if they had kept the staff they have had over recent years. Bankrupt or in the First Division? That's the gamble, and one which all of the Welsh clubs, maybe sensibly, are not willing to take. A transfer fee of half a million pounds keeps the club buoyant and financially sound for a season. If they keep the player then he may fail to bring the success to the club and Wrexham find themselves half a million pounds worse off. That is the difference between success and bankruptcy. Of all the Welsh clubs, Wrexham look the most likely to break into the First Division. For the past five seasons they have flirted with promotion and the play-offs, always stumbling at the final hurdle – in much the same way as their neighbours Tranmere Rovers have with the Premiership.

This story, the Welsh story, repeats itself around the country every season, but I challenge anyone to show me a larger, more passionate support than the Welsh clubs can muster when the signs are that success just might be around the corner. The Welsh nation thrives on passion and commitment, and yearns for success on the field. You can't always blame missed penalties and bad refs for the failure of these clubs and the national team, there is much more to the equation. Is it that we are just not good enough?

I find very little to get excited about, yet I know that many of you, and not just Welshmen, will identify with the missed opportunities that are littered around the game in Wales. Would an inquiry point the finger of blame towards the Welsh FA or to the people who have run the clubs in the past decade, the ones who no longer front the once famous clubs who play in red, white and blue? I doubt if blame would ever be clearly shared. All we really have are memories: the names, Allchurch and Charles; and the teams, Cardiff City in 1927 and Swansea City in 1981. Wrexham's Cup success stands and counts for nothing, they remain in the Second Division. Barry Town and Cwmbran Town will never bring back the thousands to the Welsh game, and in the north Bangor City have the same problems. They simply do not play at a high enough level to win a European Cup. Just take a look at the Irish for proof – always exiting the European Cups at the first or second hurdle.

There are very few positives to draw from these pages and chapters but I am sure you have found some of the tales enjoyable, and at times have smiled at the sheer lunacy that is the lower league football fan. This is what draws us all together, the spur that drives us on. I have been called a 'Northern bastard' by a ten-year-old at Orient and a 'sheep-shagger' by a fellow Welshman. It all makes me smile and I deal with much that happens with a tongue-in-cheek attitude, it gets me through the day. The characters that really matter are the lunatics who dot themselves around terraces throughout the country and shout obscure, meaningless comments at their heroes. Like the supporter who continually shouted from the Swansea North Bank, 'Toshack you're shagging me up the arse again.' Or the well-known Cardiff fan who everyone avoids because of his crazy comments from the Bob Bank. 'Play it on the floor City,' he shouts after his side has scored four headed goals. These are the ones who matter the most and I am proud to have spent some time with them because I am no different. I, too, have the 'lunatic' illness, an illness that has touched us all since the very first time some fool decided to kick a bag of wind about and try to score a goal. And if I'm ever offered a cure, I don't think I will be keeping the appointment. Some things are better left alone. Thank you for your time.

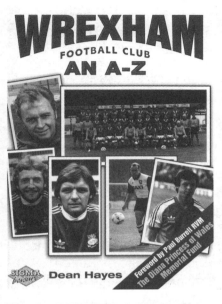

WREXHAM FOOTBALL CLUB AN A-Z

Dean Hayes

Foreword by Paul Burrell RVM
The Diana Princess of Wales
Memorial Fund

CYCLING

in **North Wales**

ABERDARON

by Philip Routledge

Wales on Horseback
Intrepid horsewoman Paula Brackston discovers Wales by horse, following many ancient pathways. £6.95

Golf Courses of North Wales
The grass is always greener and the greens are always nicer; or are they? Here's the full low-down! £9.95

Wrexham FC: An A to Z
The ideal gift for the Robins fan. Everything from Abandoned Matches to Zenith! £6.95

Postcards from the Past: Wrexham
See how this attractive town has changed over the past 100 years. £6.95

Cycling in North Wales
Easy, family routes in the most attractive parts of this stunningly beautiful area. £6.95

Cycling in South Wales
A wide collection of routes for both families and energetic solo riders. £7.95

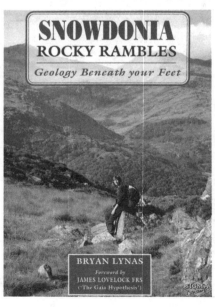